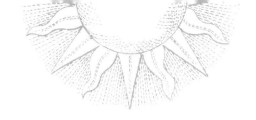

THE GREAT
HISPANIC HERITAGE

Eva Perón

THE GREAT HISPANIC HERITAGE

Isabel Allende

Simón Bolívar

Jorge Luis Borges

Miguel de Cervantes

Cesar Chavez

Roberto Clemente

Celia Cruz

Salvador Dalí

Oscar De La Hoya

Oscar de la Renta

America Ferrera

Francisco Goya

Ernesto "Che" Guevara

Dolores Huerta

Frida Kahlo, Second
   Edition

Jennifer Lopez

Gabriel García Márquez

José Martí

Pedro Martinez

Ellen Ochoa

Eva Perón

Pablo Picasso

Juan Ponce de León

Tito Puente

Manny Ramirez

Diego Rivera, Second
   Edition

Antonio López de Santa
   Anna

Carlos Santana

Sammy Sosa

Pancho Villa

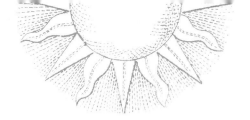

THE GREAT
HISPANIC HERITAGE

Eva Perón

Joanne Mattern

CHELSEA HOUSE
P U B L I S H E R S
An imprint of Infobase Publishing

Chelsea House
An imprint of Infobase Publishing
132 West 31st Street
New York NY 10001

Library of Congress Cataloging-in-Publication Data
Mattern, Joanne, 1963-
  Eva Perón / Joanne Mattern.
      p. cm. — (Great Hispanic heritage)
  Includes bibliographical references and index.
  ISBN 978-1-60413-729-3 (hardcover : acid-free paper) 1. Perón, Eva, 1919–1952—
Juvenile literature. 2. Argentina—History—1943-1955—Juvenile literature.
3. Women politicians—Argentina—Biography—Juvenile literature. 4. Presidents'
spouses—Argentina—Biography—Juvenile literature. I. Title. II. Series.
  F2849.P37M47 2010
  982.06'2092—dc22
  [B]   2010007812

Chelsea House books are available at special discounts when purchased in bulk quan-
tities for businesses, associations, institutions, or sales promotions. Please call our
Special Sales Department in New York at (212) 967-8800 or (800) 322-8755.

You can find Chelsea House on the World Wide Web at http://www.chelseahouse.com

Text design by Terry Mallon
Cover design by Terry Mallon/Alicia Post
Composition by EJB Publishing Services
Cover printed by Bang Printing, Brainerd, MN
Book printed and bound by Bang Printing, Brainerd, MN
Date printed: August 2010
Printed in the United States of America

10 9 8 7 6 5 4 3 2 1

This book is printed on acid-free paper.

Contents

1   **From Humble Beginnings**   6

2   **Eva's Childhood**   13

3   **A Rising Star**   21

4   **Meeting Juan Perón**   31

5   **Revolution**   40

6   **A New Argentina**   48

7   **Charity Work**   59

8   **The End**   68

9   **After Evita**   78

Chronology and Timeline   88

Notes   91

Bibliography   93

Further Reading   95

Index   97

From Humble Beginnings

The nation of Argentina was in mourning. Millions of people had been praying for weeks for God to restore the health of their First Lady, Eva Perón. Evita, as the working classes affectionately called her, was dying of cancer, and her followers, who were mostly members of labor unions and working women, were grief stricken. Crowds gathered outside the Peróns' house in the capital city of Buenos Aires, kneeling, praying, sobbing, and leaving flowers.

The crowd's tears and prayers did no good. On the evening of July 26, 1952, the government announced the sad news that Eva Perón was dead at the age of 33. When the news was announced, everything stopped. Stores and businesses closed. People walked out of restaurants and movies. They gathered in the streets, shocked at the news.

Eva's death plunged the public into a deep sorrow that the country had never witnessed before. Millions of people

Argentina mourns First Lady Eva Perón in Buenos Aires after her death in 1952. The nation's citizens were so overtaken by grief that florists sold out of their inventory and thousands of people were injured (and some killed) in the crush of the crowds gathered to pay their respects.

rushed to Buenos Aires. They piled mounds of flowers around the buildings where Eva had lived and worked. The crowds remained in the streets all day and all night, lighting candles, carrying her picture, and singing and chanting her name. The government was shocked and surprised at the reaction and wondered how to handle the huge crowds. Indeed, there was such a crush of people that several were killed and many were injured.

When the government announced that Eva's body would lie in state at the Ministry of Labor, millions of people went to view it. For two weeks, crowds lined up day and night to pay their respects. It seemed like the entire nation was in deep mourning for its beautiful and charismatic first lady.

However, not everyone mourned Eva's death. There were a number of people who were quite relieved and happy that she had passed away. Members of Argentina's upper classes had long hated Eva and her husband, President Juan Perón. They had spent years denouncing the couple and claiming that they were enriching themselves while they destroyed Argentina. Now that Eva was gone, these members of the upper classes hoped that soon Juan Perón would be gone, too, and they could regain control of their country from workers and labor unions.

Who was Eva Perón? Why did she inspire such powerful and raw feelings among the people of Argentina? For years, stories and rumors circulated about her life. These stories were called the "white myth" and the "black myth" because they portrayed her in such different lights. How could one woman be considered both the devil and a saint? It is a tribute to Eva's power and personality that she is still considered one of the most influential and fascinating figures in Latin American history.

LIFE ON THE PAMPAS

Maria Eva Duarte was born in Los Toldos, Argentina. Although records of her early life were mysteriously destroyed in the

1940s, most historians believe that Eva was born on May 7, 1919.

Los Toldos was a tiny town in the middle of the pampas. The pampas are grasslands located in the central part of Argentina that cover about one-fifth of the country. The eastern part of the pampas is covered with rich soil that is perfect for agriculture. Other parts of the pampas are perfect for raising giant herds of beef cattle. Railroads run through the pampas, linking the farming and ranching sites to the city of Buenos Aires, where goods are processed and sold. Small towns sprouted up along the railroad, and one of these towns was Los Toldos.

Eva was the youngest of five children born to Juan Duarte and Juana Ibarguren. Juan and Juana were not married; in fact, Juan had a wife and other children living in a different town. Eva had three older sisters named Blanca, Elisa, and Erminda, and an older brother named Juan.

The arrangement between Juan Duarte and Juana Ibarguren was not unusual. Ibarguren was part Indian, and at that time, many rural settlers lived with Indian women, had families with them, and then left them behind as they moved on when they had to find work or other opportunities in another town.

ARGENTINA'S GEOGRAPHY

Argentina is the second-largest country in South America. It is located near the center of the continent. Argentina is surrounded by the Atlantic Ocean on the east and the Andes Mountains and the country of Chile on the west. Brazil lies to the north. Argentina extends south all the way to the tip of the South American continent. Argentina has a variety of geographical landforms, from the steep Andes in the west to the broad, flat pampas in the center of the country.

For a while, Duarte supported his family in Los Toldos in fine style. He managed a large farm for wealthy landowners. The farm was successful, and Duarte was paid with a share of the profits. He also owned his own land, along with a car and a house. These benefits were very unusual for a farm manager.

In addition to managing the farm, Duarte was an important figure in Los Toldos. He served as the justice of the peace, settling minor arguments and legal issues for residents. Duarte's home was a popular place to gather and was often filled with neighbors who enjoyed the family's parties.

A SHOCKING CHANGE

During the early years of the twentieth century, it was good to be a wealthy landowner in Argentina. For years, the upper class controlled Argentina's government. When they were in power, life for them was comfortable and rich. Juan Duarte benefited from this power.

However, the landowners kept control through fraud and violence. They threatened voters or paid them money to vote a certain way. Finally, in 1910, Argentina's Congress decided it was time to make the government more honest. It passed laws that called for secret ballots and other voting reforms. From then on, people could vote however they liked, without anyone knowing whom they voted for. Because votes were secret, it was useless to bribe or threaten people.

By 1919, the election reforms had changed the balance of power in Argentina. During that year, a group called the Radical Party gained control of the province of Buenos Aires, where Los Toldos was located. For the first time, the rich oligarchy was not in control.

For Juan Duarte and his "second family" in Los Toldos, the change in government was a disaster. Duarte's employers suddenly had a lot less political influence. Their business got worse and profits fell. Duarte was no longer making enough money managing his farm, so he left and found a job

Juan Perón pays his last respects to his wife Eva.

managing a smaller farm nearby. But that job did not work out, either.

Then Juan Duarte made a shocking and desperate decision. In 1920, he left Juana Ibarguren, their five children, and life in Los Toldos forever. Duarte moved back to his other family in the town of Chivilcoy. Eva was less than a year old and had no memories of her father. She never saw Juan Duarte again.

GROWING UP POOR

After Juan Duarte left the family, it fell to Juana Ibarguren to support herself and her children. Without Duarte's support, the family had to leave their fine house in the center of town and move to a tiny shack near the railroad tracks. Their new home had only two rooms, plus a shed in the back for cooking and a small yard. The family had once had a maid and had enjoyed fine meals and nice clothes. Now they had to work hard and struggle for everything in their lives. Eva's older sister Erminda later wrote, "From that time on, the problem of survival became a struggle which took on a new aspect each day."[1]

To support her family, Juana Ibarguren sewed clothes for the townspeople on a small sewing machine in her house. She worked all day and all night. Soon she became ill and her legs became covered with ulcers and sores. When the local doctor told her she had to rest her legs, Ibarguren replied, "I have no time. If I rest, how can I work, how can we survive?"[2]

A lack of money was not the only thing that made life more difficult for the family. When their father was there, Eva and her siblings had been the children of a respected and important citizen. After Juan Duarte left, they were viewed as second-class citizens. The children were not only poor, but also illegitimate, or the offspring of a couple who never married. Other families in town would not let their children play with the Duarte children. Instead, Eva and her family dealt with vicious gossip.

Years later, when Eva grew up, she hated being treated without respect and held a grudge against wealthy people who acted like she was not as good as they were. Author Mary Main, who lived in Argentina during the Perón era and wrote extensively about Eva, noted that Eva "was taught from the beginning that life was a struggle for survival in which the prizes went to the toughest and the most unscrupulous; that she could afford to give advantage to none and that man was her natural enemy or a fool whom a clever girl could exploit. . . . Her indignation [about the poverty in the world] has a ring of sincerity; but it is likely that it was directed against the injustices from which she suffered herself, for she must have hated the shabby clothes that she was forced to wear and the shoddy house where they lived."[3] This anger at the class system would play an important part in her career and her life.

Eva's Childhood

Eva's childhood continued to be very difficult. Her mother sewed clothes to earn money, working such long hours that her health suffered. The children did not go hungry, since meat was cheap and plentiful on the pampas and it was easy to make such staple dishes as *puchero*, a stew made of meat, sausages, vegetables, and rice. Even worse than the poverty, however, must have been the low status that an abandoned mother and her illegitimate children faced when their protector, Juan Duarte, left town.

SIMPLE PLEASURES

Eva and her brother and sisters, like other poor children in the area, had to make their own fun. They spent many hours playing in the fields that surrounded Los Toldos, climbing trees and playing hide-and-seek, hopscotch, tag, and other outdoor games. Toys were homemade dolls or balls. Watching the trains pull in and out of the station was daily entertainment, and the children spent a lot of time watching the people who came and went or the cargo that was unloaded from the freight trains.

Most important of all was the children's imaginations. Eva and her siblings spent hours creating circuses and plays or putting on concerts for each other, using homemade costumes to transform themselves into different characters.

Since most of the other children in Los Toldos were not allowed to play with the Duartes because of their low social status, Eva and her sisters and brother played with each other. They were a close, tightly knit family. Eva was especially close to her sister Erminda, who was nearest in age to her. Their brother, Juan, enjoyed making things for the girls. He made kites and playhouses, and once even created a piano with moving keys. The oldest girls, Elisa and Blanca, told bedtime stories to the younger children.

When she was eight years old, Eva started school. Like all other girls in Argentina at the time, she put on a white smock over her dress as a school uniform. The school had only one teacher, but the students learned a wide variety of subjects, including math, literature, chemistry, and history.

Eva was an average student who rarely spoke in class and never caused any trouble. She often missed school because of illnesses. Classmates remembered her as a loner, a small and scrawny girl with very intense eyes who did not have many friends.

THE DEATH OF JUAN DUARTE

On January 8, 1926, when Eva was six years old, her family received word that Juan Duarte had been killed in a car accident in Chivilcoy. Juana Ibarguren was determined to attend the funeral, even though the presence of Duarte's "second family" could be considered an insult to his legitimate wife and children. Juana dressed her children in black mourning clothes and rushed to Chivilcoy. It was the first time Eva had ever left Los Toldos.

When the family arrived, Duarte's wake was already going on. Juana knocked on the door and told Duarte's first wife, Estela Grisolia de Duarte, who she and the children were. Estela refused to let the family in, and the two women began to argue. Estela's brother was the mayor of Chivilcoy, and Juana begged him to let her and the children enter. He finally agreed and told his sister to let the ragged family inside.

The mayor led Juana and the children into the house, where Juan Duarte's body was laid out in an open coffin. As the other guests stood and stared, Eva and her siblings walked up to the coffin and had a brief, last look at their father. Then the family went outside to wait for the funeral procession. Soon, the coffin was brought outside and placed on a horse-drawn hearse.

Duarte's first family walked directly behind the hearse in the position of honor reserved for family members. Juana and her children were allowed to walk in the procession, but they had to walk near the back of the line, with mourners who were not related to Duarte. The procession made its way to the cemetery, where a priest said a few prayers. Dirt was shoveled on the coffin, and the funeral was over. Eva and her family went home to Los Toldos.

Even though she was very young, it is likely that the treatment she received at her father's funeral hurt Eva deeply. The emotional day brought home the reality that Eva and her family lived every day: that they were not as good as other people because they were poor and illegitimate. Although Eva never wrote or spoke about her father's funeral, she did later say, "As far as I can remember the existence of injustice has hurt my soul as if a nail was being driven into it. From every period of my life I retain the memory of some injustice tormenting me and tearing me apart."[4]

MOVING TO JUNIN

After Juan Duarte died, his "second family" continued their lives in Los Toldos. However, Eva's sisters were now old

Eva Perón rose from an impoverished childhood to become a working actress and then First Lady of Argentina. She achieved iconic status due to her wild popularity among the underclass and has been immortalized onstage, in books, and on film.

enough to leave school and go to work. In 1930, the oldest, Elisa, got a job in the post office in the town of Junin, about 20 miles (32 kilometers) away from Los Toldos. Although Junin was a small community, it was a larger town than Los Toldos. Juana decided to move her family to Junin.

Eva and her family settled into a small house called a villa. The villa had an outdoor patio, and it was much nicer than the shack they had lived in while in Los Toldos. Soon afterward, Eva's sister Blanca got a job as a teacher, and her brother, Juan, became a traveling salesman for a company that made soap, floor wax, and cleaning supplies. With three of the children working, the family finally had enough money so that Juana could quit her sewing job and find a different job that was less demanding.

Juana quickly realized that there were no restaurants in Junin, so she decided to start a small one in her home. She called herself the "Widow Duarte," which gave her and her family a more respectable presence than they'd had in Los Toldos. Juana was a good cook, and soon unmarried men and widowers were coming to her house for dinner almost every night. Juana's guests included lawyers, army officers, and other respectable citizens. The men sat together at a table in the small front room, while Juana cooked and her daughters cleared the table and did the dishes. Later, two of these men would marry Eva's sisters Elisa and Blanca.

Eva was 11 years old when the family moved to Junin, and she continued her studies at the local school. One teacher remembered her as "a very beautiful little girl with dark hair and skin like porcelain, a self-absorbed child with an intense inner life, great sensitivity, and great vulnerability."[5]

Eva was quiet in school, and she still had few friends. As in Los Toldos, many parents did not let their children play with her. One child who was allowed to play with her was a girl named Elsa, an orphan being raised by two aunts who liked Eva. The two girls spent many happy times together.

As a poor, illegitimate girl, Eva became enamored with the glamour of the silver screen. It was the escape the movie theater provided that drove her into show business, although her life would become much more than acting.

THE LURE OF THE MOVIES

One of Eva's and Elsa's favorite pastimes was to go to the movies. Junin had two movie theaters, and they often showed American and European films. Eva was fascinated with the glamorous fantasy world she saw in these movies. She was especially fond of a beautiful American actress named Norma Shearer.

Eva spent as much time as she could watching movies and losing herself in a world that was very different, and much more exciting, than her life in Junin. Instead of dusty streets and simple houses, Eva saw a world with brightly lit, glittering cities and people who dressed in beautiful clothes and lived in houses filled with extravagant furniture. Eva thrilled to the excitement of these stories, especially tales of romance and adventure.

NORMA SHEARER

Norma Shearer was a popular American movie actress of the 1920s and 1930s. She was born in Canada in 1902 and won a beauty contest at age 14. In 1920, her mother took to New York to try out for the Ziegfield Follies, a popular chorus line and dance show of the time. Shearer didn't pass the audition, but she did win small parts in silent movies. In 1927, Shearer married legendary producer and studio head Irving Thalberg. After their son and daughter were born, Thalberg wanted Shearer to stay home, but she demanded bigger roles onscreen instead. Shearer appeared in many of Thalberg's films until his untimely death of heart disease in 1936. She was nominated for six Academy Awards and won the award for Best Actress for her 1930 film, *The Divorcee*. Shearer was known for her distinctive cross-eyed stare. She took great care in her appearance, swimming every day and enjoying frequent massages. Shearer retired from acting in 1942 and was rarely seen in public after that. She died in California in 1983.

When she wasn't watching movies, she and Elsa pored over movie magazines. Their favorite was *Sintonia*, which was filled with photos of the stars that the girls could cut out and save. Eva often arranged to do chores for her sister Erminda in exchange for a few of Erminda's movie star photos.

Later, Eva would recall her fascination with the lifestyles she saw onscreen: "In the place where I spent my childhood, there were more poor people than rich, but I made myself believe that there were other places in my country and in the world where things could happen in some other way . . . I imagined, for instance, that large cities were marvelous places where only wealth existed; and everything I heard about them from other people confirmed this belief. They talked about the great city as if it were a wonderful paradise where everything was beautiful and outstanding."[6] It would not be long before Eva decided that she wanted to move to the big city and become an actress. By the time she was 15, she was ready to leave Junin forever.

3

A Rising Star

Eva had always enjoyed entertaining. When she was little, she and her siblings often put on shows, concerts, or circuses for fun. She and her sisters transformed themselves into clowns by rubbing wet crepe paper on their faces for color, or they walked on a pipe held up by two sawhorses to pretend they were acrobats.

When she was a little older, Eva and her sister Erminda often visited a local disabled woman. The girls would dance and sing to entertain the woman. Eva also used her talents in school. On rainy days when the students could not play outside, Eva often entertained the younger students by reading stories and poems to them.

When she was 15 years old, Eva began performing at local poetry readings. She was an excellent and dramatic speaker, and the encouragement she received only made her more determined to leave home and become an actress. However, it would take many arguments and the help of outsiders to make Eva's dream come true.

LOCAL APPEARANCES

Eva's first public performances were at Junin's public school. In those days before television, schoolchildren often performed in public, reading poetry or excerpts from literature or dramas. Eva became a regular at these school performances, reading sentimental poetry that was the perfect showcase for her dramatic and emotional style of acting.

Eva's family thought her desire to be an actress was just a foolish dream. Her sister Blanca later explained, "Even as a child, she had shown remarkable artistic talent. In the beginning, we believed that her desire to be an actress was only a childhood dream. But her stubbornness in fighting for her dream led to lots of problems at home."[7]

Eva found a new outlet for her dramatic ambitions when Erminda joined her secondary school's cultural and arts center. The center's main purpose was to put on plays. Even though Eva did not attend secondary school yet, Erminda convinced the center's leaders to let her little sister appear in some of the plays.

Junin had a music store called Prime Arini's Music Store. The store's owner often set up loudspeakers and allowed customers to read or speak over them to entertain passersby. One Saturday, 15-year-old Eva went to the store and read several poems over the loudspeaker. Hearing her voice broadcast through the town square was exhilarating for the star-struck teenager. Eva dreamed that one day her voice would be heard on radio stations and in movies all over Argentina.

Eva also met a few professional entertainers. Occasionally, magicians and theater companies passed through Junin and performed there. Eva went to as many of these performances as she could and always hung around backstage so she could meet the actors and listen to their stories.

One day, Eva met a traveling tango singer named Agustin Magaldi, one of the most popular singers in 1930's Argentina. Magaldi sang popular, sweet, romantic songs and was known as "The Sentimental Voice of Buenos Aires." He was very handsome and charismatic, and Eva was quickly attracted to his charm. Eva asked Magaldi to take her to Buenos Aires, the capital of Argentina and the largest city in the nation. Although some biographies say that Magaldi did take Eva to Buenos Aires, many other accounts contradict this story. Although Magaldi was no doubt flattered by his young admirer, he was married and took his wife on tour with him, so it is not likely that he would want to become involved with a teenage girl. However, he did encourage Eva to follow her dreams and gave her advice about life as an entertainer in the big city. Magaldi may also have provided letters of introduction to help Eva meet important people in Buenos Aires who might be willing to give her a chance.

A NEW LIFE

Eva's dream of leaving Junin and traveling to Buenos Aires became stronger than ever. She constantly asked her mother to bring her to Buenos Aires, but Juana refused. She was worried about leaving her daughter in the big city and felt it was much safer and more sensible for Eva to stay home in Junin and build a life for herself there.

Other people had different ideas. One day, Juana talked to Jose Alvarez Rodriguez, a family friend who was the rector, or principal, of the National School of Junin. Rodriguez told Juana she should let Eva go to Buenos Aires. He believed that parents should never try to prevent their children from achieving their dreams. He said, "If the child has talent, you must let her try her wings; if she does not, you will return home happy that you supported her."[8] Juana was not thrilled with Rodriguez's advice, but she respected him enough to listen.

Early in 1935, 15-year-old Eva and her mother took the train to Buenos Aires. The two visited every radio station in the city, and Eva recited poetry at each one. The radio directors all said nice things about her talent, but no one had a job to offer her.

Finally, one station offered Eva a small part as an actress in one of their radio programs. That evening, Eva's sisters, listening at home, were startled to hear Eva's voice coming over

ARGENTINE TANGO

The dance known as the tango began in working-class neighborhoods in Buenos Aires and the city of Montevideo, Uruguay, during the late nineteenth century. At this time, immigrants from all over the world settled in Argentina and brought their dancing styles to Buenos Aires. These styles soon combined to create a new form of dance. The tango combines techniques from a Cuban dance called the *habanera* and Uruguayan dances called the *milonga* and the *candombe*, and it also includes elements of African dance music.

At first, the tango was popular only in the dance halls of Buenos Aires's lower-class neighborhoods, but its fame soon spread throughout Argentine society. The dance was featured in balls and theater performances, and its popularity spread from city neighborhoods out into the suburbs and countryside, and from the lower classes throughout all levels of society.

Tango was so popular that between 1903 and 1910 more than one-third of all records sold were of tango music. The tango was featured on 2,500 of the 5,500 records released between 1910 and 1920.

The tango spread to Europe in 1912 when dancers and musicians from Buenos Aires and Montevideo toured in Europe. The tango was introduced to the United States in 1913. Because the tango involved close dancing and lots of touching, the dance was thought to be shocking and scandalous by many people in Europe and the United States. However, its popularity continued to rise throughout the world.

The most popular tango singer in Argentine was Carlos Gardel. He recorded his first tango song, "Mi Noche Triste" ("My Sad Night"), in 1917. Gardel's sad lyrics about a doomed love affair set a standard,

the radio, reading a poem called "Where Do the Dead Go?" The director of the station, Pablo Osvaldo Valle, offered Eva a job. The salary was small, but it was enough for Eva to live on. Juana made arrangements for Eva to stay with family friends in Buenos Aires and then returned home alone. Juana was not

and most tango songs featured sentimental, romantic lyrics about love, loneliness, and the difficulties of everyday life.

In the traditional tango style, partners dance very close together, with their chests touching. A more modern open style has the partners dancing at arm's length, which allows dancers to add fancy steps and turns. Dancers generally keep their feet close to the floor as they walk, with the ankles and knees brushing as one leg passes the other. Couples dance counterclockwise around the dance floor. Because Argentine tango relies heavily on improvisation, it is very important that partners communicate with each other so that their dance flows smoothly.

The tango was extremely popular during the Perón era. Its popularity declined during the 1950s because of economic problems and a ban against public gatherings by the military dictatorships. The dance lived on in smaller venues until its revival in the 1980s following the opening in Paris of a show called *Tango Argentino* and a Broadway musical called *Forever Tango*. Today, the tango is enjoying renewed fame all over the world, partly because of the popularity of television shows such as *Dancing with the Stars*. Argentines continue to be very proud of their national dance.

happy with how things had turned out. Her daughter Blanca recalled that "Mother returned alone to Junin, furious with the Rector, furious with everyone."[9]

A STRUGGLING ACTRESS

For the next few years, Eva struggled to build a career as an actress. She quickly discovered that the life of a young performer was far from glamorous. The pay was barely enough to live on. Marcus Zucker, an actor who appeared in many productions with Eva and became good friends with her, recalled that "Those years were tremendously difficult and many young girls starting off in the theater needed help. When we were jobless, we knew sacrifice and even hunger. Both Eva and I barely made enough money to survive."[10] Zucker also recalled a day when he offered to buy Eva a cup of coffee, and

BUENOS AIRES

Buenos Aires is not only the capital of Argentina, but also one of the most important cities in South America. The city was originally founded in 1536, but was abandoned a few years later. A permanent settlement was founded in 1580. Because of its location on the Rio de la Plata, Buenos Aires quickly became a major transportation hub for shipping beef, grain, and leather goods from Argentina's interior to locations all over the area via water routes and, later, the railroads.

By the early 1900s, Buenos Aires boasted a reputation as a center of European-style culture, partly because of the large number of European immigrants who moved there. The city became a center of literature, theater, music, film, and nightlife, and has remained so to this day.

By the 1930s, Buenos Aires had become the movie capital of Latin America. Film production companies in that city made about 30 films a year, and these movies were distributed all over the Spanish-speaking countries of South and Central America.

Eva Perón moved away from her family to Buenos Aires, Argentina's capital. It was in Buenos Aires that Eva's acting career eventually took off, and it was there she met Juan Perón.

his hungry friend asked if the coffee could come with milk and a sandwich.

Actors were also considered second-class citizens by many members of society. Most parents would not let their children become actors unless the family really needed money. The situation was especially difficult for young women, who were often taken advantage of by men. Many parents would wait by the theater door to escort their daughters home immediately after a performance, in order to keep them safe and uphold their reputations.

In 1936, 17-year-old Eva found work in a theatrical company that toured Argentina. She quickly discovered that the touring life was not glamorous at all. One theater critic, Edmundo Guibourg, described how actors in these companies were "picked up, hustled around, treated like cannon fodder."[11] Only the lead actors stayed in fancy hotels; everyone else lived in cheap rooming houses, often with several actresses sharing one small room. Actors were paid very little, and they had to purchase their own costumes. They were not paid for rehearsals. If the company went out of business, the actors were not paid at all, and it was up to them to find the money to go back to Buenos Aires.

There is no doubt, however, that Eva and her fellow performers worked hard. In one town alone, the company performed its shows 43 times in just a few weeks. When Eva returned to Buenos Aires, she looked for another theater company. Over the next few years, she appeared with several other touring groups. Eva also continued to do radio work and appeared in small parts in a few movies. In 1939, Eva started her own theater company with a partner named Pascual Pelliciotta. The group was called the Company of the Theater of the Air. It won contracts with several major radio companies. From 1943 to 1945, Eva produced and starred in a series of biographical radio programs called *The Biographies of Illustrious Women*.

MAKING CONNECTIONS

Eva was pretty and she dressed as well as she could on her tiny salary. She was quick to make friends with anyone who might influence her career, from older, more successful actresses to the men who ran radio stations or theater companies. One of her favorite places to spend time was the office of *Sintonia*, the movie magazine. Eva became friends with the magazine's editor, Emilio Kartulowicz. He often mentioned her in the magazine's gossip column or included a photograph of the pretty Eva with other performers.

In 1940, Eva caught the attention of a soap manufacturer who sponsored a radio program. The program featured Eva in many of its performances. Her salary rose to a respectable wage and rose even higher in subsequent productions. Eva was finally able to move out of the shabby rented rooms she shared with other actresses and get a nice apartment of her own on a street called Calle Posadas.

Eva's circle of friends got wider all the time. Her sister Elisa was dating an army officer named Major Arrieta, and he and his friends often came to small parties Eva gave at her apartment. At that time, the military was becoming more and more active in political affairs. In 1943, a military coup had ousted Argentina's president, Ramón Castillo, and put General Pedro Pablo Ramirez in his place. Ramirez began taking more

RADIO IN ARGENTINA

Argentina was one of the first nations to have a radio station, when Radio Argentina made its first broadcast in 1920, at the dawn of the radio age. Radio Argentina's first broadcast was an opera by Richard Wagner, and it was heard by approximately 20 families in Buenos Aires who had radio receivers. By 1925, there were a dozen stations in Buenos Aires alone, and about a dozen more in other parts of the country.

The 1930s were a golden age of radio in Argentina. There were three major networks: Radio El Mundo, Radio Splendid, and Radio Belgrano. These stations broadcast music, theater programs, news, and soap operas to millions of listeners around the country.

Argentine radio enjoyed freedom of speech until 1943, when the military government took control of all broadcasting. After that, the government demanded advance approval of all scripts, and radio was used as a tool for propaganda.

control of various aspects of Argentine life, including what was broadcast on the radio. Another military officer, Colonel Anibal Imbert, was given the title of directorship of posts and telegraph, which also put him in control of the radio stations. Eva knew Imbert well and did not waste any time in using her connections to get more publicity and bigger parts for herself.

By 1943, Eva was one of the best-paid radio actresses of that time. She earned up to 6,000 pesos a month. Her photos appeared regularly in all the major entertainment magazines. She had achieved her dreams of stardom, but her life was about to take a dramatic new turn.

Meeting
Juan Perón

By the end of 1943, Eva Duarte was one of the most popular and successful actresses in Argentina. At the same time, Juan Domingo Perón was a colonel in the army and a rising star in the military government. Just a month later, in January 1944, these two celebrities would cross paths and change the fate of their nation forever.

EARTHQUAKE

January 16, 1944, was a hot summer night in Buenos Aires. Early that evening, a slight tremor shook the city. People were puzzled, but the tremor did not seem serious. However, several hundred miles away, in the Andes, the earthquake was much stronger. San Juan, a town in the mountains, was destroyed, and thousands of people were killed or injured.

Argentina's government launched a major effort to help the victims of the San Juan earthquake. Officials went to

31

JUAN PERÓN

Juan Domingo Perón was born on October 8, 1895, in the town of Lobos, near Buenos Aires. Like Eva, Perón's parents were not married when he was born, although they did stay together and ultimately got married when he was a teenager. Perón's father wanted to own land, so the family moved to Patagonia, a remote area in the far south of Argentina. There the family lived and worked on several farms before they were able to buy their own farm, which they named La Portena.

Perón went to military school at the age of 16 and joined the army in 1915. For the next few years, he was stationed in a number of remote areas in Argentina. He saw the reality of poor rural life during these years, and the poverty he witnessed made a huge impression on him. Perón also saw how unfairly laborers and labor unions were treated because the army was often called in to break up strikes and maintain order. He usually sided with the laborers during these confrontations. During one strike against a factory, the business's owners had locked up the company store. Perón forced the company to open the store so desperate workers could get food and water.

examine the destruction, and soldiers were sent to the area to help. A charitable collection began in Buenos Aires, and everyone was asked to contribute.

Juan Domingo Perón was an army colonel who was the head of Argentina's department of labor. He took a strong interest in helping the victims of the earthquake. Perón came up with the idea of holding a festival to raise money. The nation's leading actors and actresses, escorted by the military, would walk the streets of Buenos Aires, carrying boxes to collect donations. A few days later, a huge benefit gala would be held, featuring dancers, comedians, musicians, and other entertainers, and money from the tickets would be used

In 1926, Perón was promoted to captain and returned to Buenos Aires. Over the next few years, he rose through the ranks, eventually becoming a colonel. He also taught military history and lectured on various topics in universities and army-run training schools.

In 1928, Perón married his first wife, Aurelia Tizon. By all reports, the couple had a happy marriage, but they never had children. Tizon died of uterine cancer in 1938. Oddly enough, the same disease would later kill Perón's second wife, Eva.

In 1939, World War II broke out in Europe, and Perón traveled to Italy to study how the army was being trained and deployed. He became an admirer of Italy's Fascist leader, Benito Mussolini, and he kept in mind the sense of order and control he had seen in Italy upon his return to Argentina in 1942.

Perón was a close friend of General Edelmiro Farrell, and when Farrell became president of Argentina in 1944, Perón was given the position of war minister. This was a prestigious post and made Perón the most influential and powerful man in the government. Perón already held the post of secretary of labor, which gave him the means to do something he had wanted to do since his days as a young army officer: give more power to the workers and the labor unions. His efforts paid off, giving the ambitious Perón a strong base that would bring him into power and remain loyal to him for many years.

to help the earthquake victims. The gala was scheduled for January 22 and would be held at Luna Park Stadium, a huge sports arena in Buenos Aires.

Eva had been one of the actresses who collected money, and she also appeared at the gala. Perón was there, too, and it was that night that Eva and Perón met for the first time. Eva later called this moment her "marvelous day,"[12] while Perón wrote that Eva came into his life "as if brought by destiny."[13]

EVA AND JUAN PERÓN

From that night on, Eva and Juan Perón were inseparable. By that time, Perón had become a rising star in Argentina's government, and Eva sensed that great things were in store for him. She was especially pleased that Perón believed in helping the people. Rather than spending all of his time with the nation's wealthy elite, or oligarchy, Perón was more interested in helping the working class and people who were less fortunate.

Perón was a strong believer in workers uniting to help their cause. He encouraged workers to form labor unions because he knew that unions would help the workers achieve a better standard of living. Before Perón came to power, only 20 percent of Argentina's work force was unionized, and most of these unions were concentrated in the railway and food-processing industries. During the 1930s, a large number of workers moved to Buenos Aires, but the unions never reached out to this new population. No one had ever tried to help these workers until Perón came along. For this reason, the workers were thrilled to have a leader who looked out for their interests, and they were very loyal to Perón. Their loyalty, in turn, helped Perón build a base of political power.

It is no surprise that Eva, who came from a poor background, was impressed and delighted with Perón's actions. In her book, *La Razon de mi Vida*, Eva wrote of Perón, "I put myself by his side . . . and when he had time to listen to me I spoke up as best I could: 'If, as you say, the cause of the people

PERÓN'S LABOR UNIONS

Labor unions had existed in Argentina for many years, but they were poorly organized and had little political power before Perón came to power. Perón built the nation's largest union, the Confederación General del Trabajo (CGT), or General Confederation of Labor, from 250,000 members to 6 million highly organized workers. With Perón's backing, union members were able to obtain higher wages and improved working conditions, and they became fiercely loyal supporters of Perón.

From the moment they met, Juan and Eva Perón bonded over their commitment to helping the underclass. Throughout their life together, Eva would serve as Juan Perón's greatest champion.

is your own cause, however great the sacrifice I will never leave your side until I die.'"[14]

On July 9, 1944, Perón and Eva were seen together for the first time in public, when they both appeared at a party. Behind the scenes, the couple was living in adjoining apartments in Eva's building on Calle Posadas.

A CLEVER ARRANGEMENT

Perón asked Eva to work with him at the labor department. He thought Eva's energy and organizational skills would be a great help in developing a labor policy for women, and he liked the idea of a woman as leader of the movement. Eva agreed but wanted to continue her work at the radio station first. For the next year and a half, Eva continued to act in and produce radio shows and appear in films.

Eva's radio career was at its highest point after she met Perón. She was offered the biggest broadcasting contract of that time: 35,000 pesos, or more than $7,500 a month, to record more of her popular *Biographies of Illustrious Women* for Radio Belgrano, one of Argentina's top broadcasting stations.

Eva also worked out a lucrative arrangement that led to her appearance in movies. Film stock was very hard to get during World War II, which was currently raging in Europe. When film did arrive in Argentina, it was delivered directly to the government. Eva used Perón and her other connections to have the film stock given to her. She, in turn, gave it to San Miguel Studios so they could make movies. It was no coincidence that these movies starred none other than Eva Duarte. For her first starring film role, in a movie called *La Cabalgata del Circo*, Eva bleached her hair blonde. She would continue to be a blonde for the rest of her life.

PROPAGANDA FOR THE PEOPLE

Eva wasted no time in using her own celebrity to help Perón. Every night on the radio, she broadcast programs that talked about Perón's great qualities and how he had made life better for the poor working people.

Eva often spoke as a character called simply "The Woman." "The Woman" spoke of the triumphs of the military revolution and constantly gave Perón most of the credit for the changes in society. "There was a man who could bring dignity to the notion of work, a soldier of the people who could feel the flame of social justice . . . it was he who decisively helped the people's Revolution,"[15] Eva proclaimed in a typical broadcast.

Eva had no previous experience with politics, but she spoke to the people as an ordinary woman, and she was able to help people feel the great respect and love she had for Perón. More people voiced their support of Perón. Many more joined the labor unions that were springing up in many different industries in Buenos Aires. One of these new unions was the Agrupación Radial Argentina, a group of actors and radio performers. Eva became its president in 1944.

THE FORCES AGAINST EVA AND PERÓN

While the workers and the unions idolized Perón and were fascinated by Eva, not everyone in Argentina felt this way. Members of the oligarchy, or the ruling upper class, did not like Perón and Eva at all. They felt threatened by so much power being handed to the working class and the poor, and they feared what would happen to their social class if Perón ever became the nation's president.

Members of the oligarchy also looked down on Eva. They resented the fact that an illegitimate girl who had grown up in disgrace and poverty was now the girlfriend of one of the most powerful men in Argentina. In the extremely class-conscious society that was present in Argentina at the time,

THE CATHOLIC CHURCH IN ARGENTINA

The Roman Catholic religion has always been a very important part of politics, law, and culture in Argentina. Until the country's constitution was changed in 1994, Argentina's two top leaders were required to be Roman Catholic. Argentine law and society reflected the church's traditional values. Today, more than 90 percent of Argentina's population still considers itself Catholic.

Eva used her influence as a radio personality to broadcast propaganda to the public. She spoke from her heart about Juan Perón's potential for changing the country, and as a result, she succeeded in gaining a following for the rising military leader.

it was shocking for someone of Eva's background to be considered equal to—or even better than—families who'd had money and power for generations.

The oligarchy began to spread rumors about Eva's character, saying she was immoral. They asked why she and Perón did not get married and criticized them for living together, which was against the beliefs of the Catholic Church, Argentina's official church. Eva tried to ignore these insults, but she often spoke out against them in her radio speeches. She criticized anyone who did not support Perón as an enemy of the nation.

Perón also faced troubles within the government. Other members of the military were not happy with his increasing fame and power. The military government in Argentina was very unstable, and presidents seemed to come and go almost overnight. In 1945, a group of army officers who were unhappy with President Ramirez visited him in the middle of the night and forced him at gunpoint to retire from the presidency. Ramirez agreed, and two weeks later, Colonel Edelmiro Farrell became the nation's new president. Farrell appointed Perón, who was a good friend of his, to a new office as minister of war. Because Farrell did not seem to be in charge despite his title, many people felt that Perón was really the one who was in charge of the government. Later, Farrell named Perón vice president.

Other officers became very nervous at the amount of power Perón had suddenly acquired. Perón's support of the workers had a darker side because he was opposed to members of the other classes. During this time, newspapers who spoke against the government were closed down, and opposition leaders were arrested and tortured. Anyone who spoke against the government faced danger.

During the time, most of the world was fighting against Adolf Hitler and the Nazis who controlled Germany. Many people felt that Perón was a Nazi, or at the very least, wanted to have the same dictatorial powers that Hitler possessed. These fears helped unite many political groups and give them one clear focus: to get rid of Juan Perón.

5

Revolution

By 1945, many political groups had united against Juan Perón. The country seemed to be divided into two groups: those who admired and supported Perón and those who hated him. Tension built over the months. Finally, in October 1945, that tension exploded into action.

PERÓN'S ARREST

On October 8, 1945, a group of army officers asked Juan Perón to resign from his government positions. When he refused, the officers went to President Farrell and told him that if Perón did not resign, troops would march on the city and overthrow the entire government. Faced with this threat, Farrell had no choice but to tell Perón to resign. Perón had no choice, either. He resigned from his government posts and also resigned from the army. On that same day, Radio Belgrano officials fired Eva from her position at the radio station.

If the military leaders thought that Perón and Eva would disappear after their loss of power, they were wrong. The day after his resignation, Perón made a farewell speech that was broadcast on the radio. The government was not happy about this and decided the best way to silence Perón was to place him under arrest. On October 13, Perón was arrested and sent to a naval fortress on Martin Garcia, an island off the coast near Buenos Aires. The officers told Perón that this action was meant to protect his life, but everyone knew the real truth.

Perón was nervous about being in the navy's hands since he had many more friends in the army than in the navy. Eva reportedly cried most of the way back to Buenos Aires and clung to Perón's arm until the officers pushed her away.

DAYS OF FEAR AND ACTION

No one knew what would happen to Perón, least of all Eva. She was determined to get Perón out of prison, but in reality, she had no real power. Without Perón's support, Eva was just an out-of-work actress with a few friends in high places. She did not know what to do. Years later, Eva wrote, "Those eight days still cause me pain—greater, far greater than anything I would have experienced had I spent them in his company, sharing his pain. . . . I went out in the streets, looking for friends who might still accomplish something on his behalf. . . . I never felt—and I mean this—quite so small, so utterly unimportant as I did during those eight memorable days."[16]

Eva tried to get Perón out of jail. She went to see a lawyer and asked him to request Perón's release formally before a judge, but the lawyer refused. Eva's other friends were no help, either. It looked like Perón's fate was out of her hands.

Perón was also worried and feeling lonely in his island prison. On October 14, Eva received a letter from Perón, delivered by their friend Colonel Miguel Angel Mazza. Mazza was an army doctor who had been allowed to visit Perón in prison. The letter proclaimed how much he loved and missed her and also hinted at his hopes for the future. Perón wrote, "I have asked Farrell for a quick discharge. When I get out, we'll get married and go anywhere to live in peace."[17]

Mazza also gave the newspapers a letter that Perón had written to President Farrell, demanding his release. However, the newspapers, which were not friendly to Perón, printed only parts of the letter. Once again, efforts to help Perón seemed useless.

DAY OF REVOLUTION

The government hoped that, with Perón out of the picture, people would forget about him. However, they had not counted on the labor unions. Members of the working class had always been Perón's biggest supporters, and they worried what would happen to their new power if Perón's enemies came into power.

On October 15, several labor leaders met and called for a strike. Even before the official proclamation, smaller strikes had broken out in factories around the city. A general strike was set for October 17.

While the workers struggled to find a way to make their voices heard, Colonel Mazza was also working to free Perón. He claimed the general was ill with a lung disease called pleurisy and produced some old X-rays to fool the navy into believing him. After much argument and discussion, the navy agreed to move Perón from Martin Garcia to a guarded hospital room in Buenos Aires. Eva was not particularly cheered by this news. Although Perón was back in the city, he was still a prisoner. To calm her down, Mazza arranged for Eva to speak to Perón, who told her to be calm and stay out of danger. On October 17, the day of the general strike, she was to stay home. Eva agreed.

On October 17, thousands of workers did not go to their jobs. Instead, they marched through the streets and gathered in the Plaza de Mayo in the center of town. Witnesses described the happy, nonviolent mood of the crowd and how they

A crowd gathers in opposition to Juan Perón in 1945. Perón's fervent support of the lower class gained him many enemies in the upper class. As his political career rose during a troubled time in Argentina, he also became more vulnerable to losing everything.

shouted and sang. Soon, an estimated crowd of 200,000 people stood in front of the president's residence, the Casa Rosada, shouting and waving signs. They demanded that Perón be freed. The city was paralyzed, and the military government had no choice. They had to give in to the workers and free Perón.

At 11 o'clock that night, a jubilant Perón appeared on the balcony of the Casa Rosada. The crowd below him held up torches made of lit newspapers and called his name. Argentine historian Felix Luna described the odd mood that night. "People seemed to have lost their minds; they cried out, they jumped up and down, they wept and shouted their slogans, getting hoarser and hoarser. Here was the man on whose behalf they had acted and he was safe and sound and triumphant."[18]

Perón stood on the balcony for 15 minutes before the cheering died down enough for him to speak. He announced that he had resigned from the army and from now on would work only for the people of Argentina. "I want to mix with this sweating mass as a simple citizen," he said. "I want to hug it close to my heart as I would my mother."[19]

EVA'S ROLE IN THE REVOLUTION

People who were opposed to Perón were dumbfounded by this turn of events. Never before had the working class won the release of their leader and then seen him returned to power. Many people were convinced that Eva was behind Perón's freedom and reinstatement into power. Some historians have promoted this view, saying that Eva organized the general

ARGENTINA'S "PINK HOUSE"

Casa Rosada means "Pink House" in Spanish. The building is probably the most photographed and well-known location in Buenos Aires. Rumor has it that the building's pink color was a long-ago compromise between two warring political parties, one whose symbol was the color red and the other whose symbol was the color white. The two colors were combined to create pink.

Located on the east end of the large, open Plaza de Mayo, the Casa Rosada is officially known as the Casa de Gobierno, or Government House. Although many people think the president of Argentina lives in the Casa Rosada, the truth is that he or she only works there. The Casa Rosada's balcony has served as a public speaking place for almost every Argentine president, as well as for other famous historical figures, such as Pope John Paul II—and, of course, Eva Perón.

strike and was instrumental in uniting the working class and seeing that they freed Perón.

In truth, most evidence shows that Eva had very little to do with the events of October 17. Perón himself had told her to stay home that day in order to ensure her safety. Several labor leaders also assert that Eva had nothing to do with the general strike and the march on the Casa Rosada. Cipriano Reyes, the leader of the Labor Party at that time, adamantly denied that Eva had enough power to have anything to do with the revolution. "At that moment she had no labor union experience and had no contact with the workers nor the public, and even less with our strike committee," he stated.[20]

Father Hernan Benitez, a close friend and Eva's confessor, agreed with Reyes. "It's a fact that Eva had no role in the events of October 17th. That day was mainly the work of Cipriano Reyes."[21]

Although Juan Perón later gave Eva some credit for his release, Eva herself was quick to give all credit to the people. "That week of October 1945 is a week of many shadows and of many lights," she later wrote. "It would be better if we did not come too close . . . However, this does not impede me from saying . . . that the light came only from the people."[22]

NEW BEGINNINGS

Five days after the revolutionary events that freed Perón, he made good on his promise to Eva. On October 22, the two were married in a private civil ceremony. Five weeks later, they had a religious ceremony at the Church of San Ponciano in La Plata. The marriage contract had several mistakes, including the wrong birth date for Eva. She had stated that she was born in 1922, not 1919.

After his marriage and a short honeymoon, Perón set about the business of running for Argentina's president. The Labor Party chose him as its candidate, and a number of other groups also came to his side. His opposition was made up of a mixed group of conservatives, radicals, and other political parties. This party was very organized and had a lot of money, while Perón's campaign had very little of either. What he did have was his new wife. Although Eva rarely spoke on behalf of

Eva accompanied her new husband on his campaign journeys throughout the country. Above, the couple greets supporters at a stop. This began the public's fascination with Eva Perón.

Perón at this time, she was constantly at his side as they traveled throughout the country. It was the first time in Argentina's history that a candidate's wife accompanied him during a campaign. At each stop, Eva handed out campaign buttons and personally greeted Perón's supporters. People were fascinated with this blonde beauty who had been a glamorous radio star and whose marriage seemed like a fairy tale come to life.

The presidential campaign was a nasty one, with many accusations thrown by both sides. Violence also erupted. The opposition's train faced bomb threats, attempted derailments, and physical attacks by Perón's supporters. Perón's train, called the *El Descamisado*, after the common name for the working class (*descamisados* means "shirtless ones" in English), traveled under heavy security.

The election was held on February 24, 1946. When all the votes were counted, Perón had won with 52 percent of the vote. His party's candidates had won all but one of the local elections and held 28 out of 30 seats in the Senate, as well as a two-thirds majority in the chamber of deputies. Just over three months later, on June 5, 1946, Perón was sworn in as president, making Eva the country's First Lady. Argentina was now securely in the hands of the Peróns.

6

A New Argentina

When Juan Perón took control of Argentina, the country was one of the richest nations in the world. Perón was in a unique position in that his government had plenty of money to spend. With Eva's strong encouragement, Perón chose to spend much of that money on social programs for the poor.

RICH BEYOND BELIEF

When World War II ended in 1945, it left a changed world behind. Much of Europe was devastated by bombs and battles, and the same was true in Japan, China, and other nations in the Far East. Victorious European nations, such as Great Britain, Russia, and France, faced the huge task of rebuilding cities, finding jobs for returning soldiers, and helping people whose lives and financial stability had been severely damaged by six years of war. Even the United States, which had not suffered any battles or bombings on its soil, except for the

Japanese attack on the military base of Pearl Harbor in Hawaii, had returning soldiers to take care of and was also actively involved in rebuilding Europe.

World War II left Argentina in a powerful position. Not only was the country undamaged by the war, but it also had many riches to offer the rest of the world. Europe needed beef and grain to feed its people, and Argentina had plenty of both for sale. Argentina also had enough money to lend billions of dollars to European nations. At one point, Great Britain alone owed Argentina almost $2 billion.

Perón came to power during a time of unprecedented riches for his country. There was so much money coming in that he once boasted that "walking through the Central Bank's cellars was difficult because of all the gold ingots on the floor."[23]

Perón had a clear idea of how to spend some of Argentina's fortune. He wanted to make conditions better for Argentina's working class. Perón had two major reasons for this decision. He genuinely wanted to help people, and he knew that this aid would build even more political support for himself from the labor unions and the descamisados.

Under Perón's leadership, the government began nationalizing, or taking control, of many industries. The railroads were one of the first industries to be nationalized, and others soon followed. Perón also encouraged workers to form more labor unions. These unions gave the workers a voice and helped them unite into a strong force that could demand higher pay and better working conditions. Not surprisingly, most workers adored Perón for making their lives better. However, not everyone shared the workers' enthusiasm for their new leader and his wife.

UNHAPPY CITIZENS

The landowners and factory owners were not at all happy with Perón's reforms. If they had to pay their workers more, their profits went down. Giving the workers better conditions, such as shorter hours or safer procedures, also cost the landowners and factory owners a lot of money.

The oligarchy was also angry about the way things were going. They resented being ordered around by an army general and felt that the poor descamisados did not deserve to have so much power. For generations, the rich had ruled the country, and it was hard for them to accept this monumental social change.

Female members of the oligarchy were especially upset with Eva. They simply did not feel she was good enough to be a member of Argentina's highest social circle. To these woman, Eva was a lower-class, illegitimate child who had grown up to become an actress, which was then considered a scandalous profession. Seeing Eva wearing glamorous gowns and attending important social functions made them seethe with anger.

Eva was soon the target of malicious gossip from members of the upper class. One American visitor to Argentina noted that "Among the members of the oligarchy, the relating of juicy items has become almost an obsession. Many of them spent their evenings whipping themselves into hysteria by exchanging gossip about the regime."[24]

Eva sensed their resentment, and it only made her more determined to live in style. Ever since she was a child, she had been looked down upon and shunned. Now she was the First Lady of Argentina, and she refused to be treated as a second-class citizen any longer.

PARTNERS

Argentina had never seen a First Lady like Eva Perón before. Other First Ladies had stayed out of the spotlight and rarely appeared with their husbands in public. Eva had very different ideas. She was an integral part of Perón's government and saw herself as a direct connection between Perón and the people. Eva visited factories and met with workers. She went out into the streets of poor neighborhoods to see how people lived and what their needs were. Perón could not do this because of his position, but Eva could. "My mission is to transmit to the Colonel the concerns of the Argentine people," she told workers at a meat-packing plant.[25]

As First Lady, Eva stayed in touch with the people in a way that Juan Perón could not. By availing herself to the public to address labor disputes, she became a very visible member of her husband's administration.

Eva soon set up an office for herself on the fourth floor of the Central Post and Telecommunications Building. Groups of workers soon crowded into the office, asking Eva to help them solve labor disputes or win better pay. Eva's small office was soon overwhelmed by the crowds, and so was Eva. She wrote in *La Razon de mi Vida*, "Little by little, I couldn't tell you on what exact day. I can tell you that at first I took care of everything myself. Then I had to ask for help. Finally I had to organize the work which in just a few weeks had become extraordinary."[26]

On September 24, Eva moved into Perón's suite of offices at the Secretariat of Labor and Welfare. It was easier for her to work on labor issues in this department, and the office was also larger and better suited to handle the crowds of people that were now coming to see her every day.

Eva was determined to create instant solutions. Many people complained that when the government said it would do something to solve a problem, it took so long to figure out what to do and then put a plan into action that the problem only got worse while people waited for help. Eva had a much more immediate approach. If someone needed a job, she would find one for him or her. If a child were sick, she would give him or her medicine. Hungry people were immediately given food.

A good example of Eva's action occurred in January 1947. Visitors told Eva that living conditions were very poor in a slum called the Villa Soldati. Eva went to visit the area on the same day and decided that the residents needed to move to better housing. Within a week, some families were already moving into new homes, while others were transferred to emergency housing until their homes could be completed a few months later.

It was no surprise that the working class and the poor came to adore Eva even more as the weeks went by. For the first time, they had someone in power who actually cared about them and met with them face-to-face. Soon Eva had a new nickname, "Evita," given to her affectionately by the descamisados.

However, not everyone was thrilled with Eva's activities. Many people in Perón's government thought she was meddling in matters that were none of her business and interfering in their affairs. Perón's aides were angry that Perón seemed to make appointments and fire people based on what Eva wanted. There were even reports that Eva had interrupted a closed session of the Senate and then went running to Perón to complain after the senators criticized her for being there. In 1947, a report from the British labor office mentioned Eva's "interference in affairs of state . . . daily more conspicuous."[27] Eva even maneuvered Perón to hire her brother, Juan, as his private secretary, which meant that Eva knew everything that went on in Perón's office.

GLAMOUR AND PUBLICITY

Eva worked hard, but she did not spend all her time meeting with the descamisados. She and Perón attended many official

SOCIAL CLASSES IN ARGENTINA

Social classes in Argentina were very distinct and restrictive during the first half of the twentieth century. The upper class was made up of owners of large estates, along with merchants who owned large stores or other businesses and industrialists who ran factories. Many of these families had been wealthy for generations and felt they were better than other classes. The largest segment of society was the middle class, which was made up of management-level workers in the industrial, commercial, and public sectors. Members of the lower class worked as laborers on farms, factories, or railroads and usually had jobs that were very physically demanding.

functions, parties, and galas. For these occasions, Eva dressed in the latest styles, wearing glamorous dresses and covering herself with dazzling and very expensive jewelry.

Eva made sure that photographers were present to document her every move. Newspapers were filled with photos of her in beautiful gowns and jewelry, smiling as she stood beside Perón or greeted foreign dignitaries. Eva also made sure the newspaper photographers captured her working with the poor. Not a day went by that the newspapers did not carry pictures of Eva going about her work.

Eva understood that she and Perón were heroic figures to Argentina's working class and that attention should always be focused on them. To her, politics was not that different than acting. She once told a friend, "Governing is like making a film. A female lead, a male lead, and the rest, just extras."[28]

THE RAINBOW TOUR

In 1947, Spain invited Eva for an official state visit. At that time, Spain was run by a Fascist government headed by General Francisco Franco. Because the nation was run by a dictator, most other countries in Europe would not trade with Spain, and the United States would not provide any food or aid to the struggling country. As a result, many Spanish people were starving. Perón stepped in and shipped 16,000 tons of wheat to Spain. The nation was so grateful it viewed the Peróns as their saviors.

Other countries also invited Eva to visit. Soon her itinerary had expanded to include Italy, France, Switzerland, and Portugal, and the trip was called the Rainbow Tour. Eva was thrilled to go to Europe. She was the first wife of an Argentine president to be invited on an official foreign visit. A European visit was also a way to thumb her nose at the rich women of the oligarchy. At that time, European tours were very common for members of the upper classes. By traveling to Europe as an official representative of the government, Eva was doing the oligarchy one better.

Eva Perón toured Europe on an official state visit in 1947. Most European nations did not welcome her with open arms, although she was a hit in Spain. Above, Eva meets Pope Pius XII at the Vatican.

Eva and her entourage left Argentina on a plane, with another plane just to carry her clothes and jewelry taking off right behind them. The tour started triumphantly in Spain, where she spent 15 days. She met Franco and received from him the Grand Cross of Isabella the Catholic, Spain's highest honor. Eva also went to banquets, performances, and festivals held in her honor. Crowds followed her everywhere she went, and Eva made sure to carry handfuls of money to toss out to the children who crowded around her car.

In Italy, Eva met with Pope Pius XII. He gave her a gold rosary and made her an honorary member of a Franciscan religious order. However, the crowds in Italy were not as adoring as the crowds in Spain. There were several protests, and many people shouted "Down with Fascism" when Eva passed by. Along with their distrust of Perón's government policies, many people also felt that Eva's ostentatious display of wealth was insulting at a time when most of Europe was still struggling to get over the devastating effects of World War II.

Eva also visited France, Portugal, and Switzerland, but her welcome there was not as fervent as it had been in Spain. Many people did not like Perón and viewed him as a dictator. They called his style of government "Perónism" and compared it to Fascism. If Eva was disappointed about her reception in several of the European countries, she did her best to hide it.

WHAT IS FASCISM?

Fascism is government control of a nation's economy. Rather than controlling the economy directly through government ownership of businesses, which is a characteristic of Socialism, Fascist governments control the economy by dominating private owners. Business owners are required to use their property for the national industry and do whatever the government demands of them. A Fascist government also sets prices and wages. State departments, called ministries, determine what goods will be produced and how. To keep the economy running, only nationally made products are available, and imports from other countries are banned or strictly controlled.

The most famous Fascist leaders of the twentieth century were Benito Mussolini, who ruled Italy from 1922 until 1943; Francisco Franco, ruler of Spain from 1936 to 1975; and, most notoriously, Adolf Hitler, whose Nazi Party ruled Germany from 1933 until the end of World War II in 1945.

The most disappointing response came from Great Britain. Eva had hoped to go to England and visit the king and queen, and at first it seemed that she would be invited to have tea with the queen. However, Eva's arrival was delayed by two weeks, putting it squarely during the time that the royal family traditionally vacationed in Scotland. The British government sent a message saying Eva was welcome to visit Great Britain, but that the royal family would not be able to meet with her. Eva was so insulted, she decided to skip Great Britain altogether.

Eva returned to Argentina after three months in Europe. Despite its disappointments, the Rainbow Tour was promoted as a huge success. The Argentine people felt that their nation was being taken seriously at last. Proudest of all were the descamisados, who viewed Eva as their personal representative. However, the oligarchy was not impressed with Eva's exploits and said that Spain only welcomed her because of Perón's generous gifts and loans. In response, Eva and Perón warned people that the oligarchy was a dangerous enemy that could destroy everything they had worked so hard to achieve for the working class and the poor.

THE RIGHT TO VOTE

After her return from Europe, Eva got right back to work. Argentine women had been fighting for the right to vote since the early 1900s without success, and Eva made this her new passion. She made many speeches encouraging women to fight for suffrage, or the right to vote, and explaining that Argentina's working women should support her husband. Every Wednesday night, Eva broadcast a radio message urging all women to join her efforts. She also published articles in the newspapers. Behind the scenes, she visited legislators and talked to delegations of women who came to see her.

With Eva pushing for women's suffrage, Perón was quick to agree. In 1947, he encouraged Congress to pass a law giving women the right to vote. Eva was thrilled at this victory. On September 23, the day the law was passed, she told a group of female supporters, "Women of my country, I am receiving from the National Government the law that establishes our civil rights, joyfully feeling a trembling in my hands as I touch our victory laurel."[29]

Eva quickly took advantage of this new bloc of voters. In 1947, she formed a new political party, called the Perónist Women's Party. Perón was initially opposed to this new party, saying that all of his supporters, both male and female, should be united under one party's banners, but Eva was unstoppable. By 1951, when the first national election involving women was held, almost all of the 4 million women who turned out to vote supported Juan Perón. In addition, 29 women were elected to Congress and many more won offices in Argentina's provinces and towns. The face of Argentina's political parties had changed forever.

Charity Work

From her earliest days as First Lady, Eva had worked hard to help the poor. Of course, she was not the first person to give aid to the needy. However, Eva had a whole new way of doing things, and her ideas and actions quickly angered those who had been in charge of helping others before. They also led to suspicion about what was really going on behind the scenes of Eva's charitable actions.

THE BENEFICENT SOCIETY

For many years, wealthy women from the upper class had run a charity called the Sociedad de Beneficencia, or the Beneficent Society. It was founded in 1923, and in 1946, it was made up of 87 elderly upper-class ladies. The society operated several hospitals, orphanages, and homes for the elderly. Originally these endeavors were funded by donations from the women and their families themselves, but by the 1940s, they were funded by money raised from a government lottery or directly through cash grants from the national budget.

Even in 1946, the society ran things in a heavy-handed manner that made sure the poor and other recipients of their help were treated like second-class citizens. Authors Nicholas Fraser and Marysa Navarro described the conditions in a society-run orphanage in 1946: "Children at its orphanages wore blue smocks and had their heads shaved. Young women earned part of their keep by sewing clothes for the Oligarchy. Each Christmas these children had their heads shaved and were sent through the streets in dark clothes to solicit funds on the Sociedad's behalf, pathetic figures to tug at the public conscience."[30]

It was traditional for the First Lady to be the president of the society. Eva intended to fulfill this office, but the society's upper-class members were appalled at the very idea of having her in their organization. Eva's close friend Father Hernan Benitez thought there was another reason the ladies were uncomfortable with the thought of Eva as their president. "For those ladies, poor people were something unfamiliar, remote. Eva had known hunger and misery personally."[31] Eva herself was tired of the upper class's attitude toward the poor. "When the rich think about the poor, they have poor ideas," she said.[32]

Eva was also bothered by the fact that the society's ladies often used entertainment, such as concerts or parties, to raise money for the poor. To her, this was another example of "charity" that was really just exploitation. One story describes a meeting between some of the society's ladies and Eva, where the ladies told her that they planned to hold a bridge party at the Plaza Hotel and donate the money raised to the poor. Eva interrupted them, saying, "Absolutely not! You must realize that in this country the sorrows of the poor will never again serve as entertainment for the rich!"[33]

The society sent word to Eva that she could not be its president, using the excuse that she was too young. Eva was

Eva always made sure photographers were present for a photo opportunity, whether she was dressed in her finest to entertain foreign dignitaries or was spending time with the public that adored her.

hurt and angry because she knew the real reasons they were rejecting her. In response to their comments, Eva suggested that her elderly mother could take her place—a suggestion that was quickly rejected. After that, Eva shut down the society altogether. This wasn't hard to achieve, as many people in the government felt that the society's heavy-handed efforts were out of date and needed to be transformed. Eva told the ladies that Perón's government intended to replace charity with social justice, and the Beneficent Society was no more.

EVA'S FOUNDATION

Eva set about creating a new type of charity. On June 19, 1948, she founded the Eva Perón Foundation. Although Eva joked to her husband that he should donate his salary as president in order to start the foundation, she herself gave 10,000 pesos to get things rolling. The foundation had five goals: 1) to loan money, provide tools, and establish scholarships for people who lacked resources; 2) to construct houses for needy families; 3) to build schools, hospitals, recreational facilities, and any other building the foundation deemed necessary; 4) to construct buildings for the common good which could be transferred to the government; and 5) to contribute to works constructed for the common good and which helped meet the basic needs of the poor.

After Eva's initial investment, donations poured in from all over Argentina. Many of these donations were not voluntary. Eva suggested that unions, businesses, and ordinary citizens contribute money to the foundation. If people did not follow her "suggestions," they would not receive raises or they might be fined or jailed. In addition to contributions from the public, Perón's government also sent money to the foundation in a variety of ways. Whenever a national wage increase went into effect, everyone's first month's raise went to the foundation. The foundation also received one percent of the national lottery, as well as money earned from racetracks, casinos, and fines from tax evasion. Not everyone thought this was fair.

Socialist writer Americo Ghioldi said, "The Government had placed powers of coercion, of violence, and of menace in the capricious hands of the First Lady."[34]

In spite of the problems with where the money came from, Eva's foundation did a tremendous amount of good work. The foundation started temporary homes for mothers and children who came to Buenos Aires for medical treatment. The foundation also set up free medical care for the poor and funded the construction of new hospitals. Female workers in Buenos Aires could live in comfortable apartment buildings that featured private rooms, affordable restaurants, a library, a day care center, and a medical clinic. The foundation also built housing projects for workers, giving them better living conditions than the ones found in the slums where they had previously lived. Temporary homes gave homeless people a comfortable place to stay for a short time and provided a staff of social workers to help them solve their problems and find resources to get them on their feet again.

Between 1948 and 1952, the foundation built 1,000 schools and more than 60 hospitals. It trained about 1,300 nurses a year and also established homes for the elderly and for unwed mothers. Eva also created a children's city to house about 200 orphans and built special resorts where poor people could go on vacation.

Health care was an important focus of the foundation. Both Eva and Perón understood that providing good health care to everyone was an important part of creating a happy and prosperous society. In 1950, a government publication quoted Perón's frustration with the health care situation in Argentina. "In the country of meat, in the country of bread, in the country which has 300 days of sunlight a year, in the country where we have everything . . . the average life span is ten to twenty years less than Europe and ten years less than in the U.S. Organizing public health can prolong our lives an average of ten to twenty years."[35] Perón also complained about how unfair it was that a millionaire could afford to pay for the best doctors, while the poor did not have that option. To the Peróns, a strong public health care system would ensure quality care for everyone, and that is why much of the foundation's work focused on building hospitals and clinics, training nurses and doctors, and starting a mobile "health train" to reach patients who could not travel to the hospital.

Eva always had a special love for helping children. The foundation sponsored a number of youth tournaments, where children could participate in sports competitions. All the fees, uniforms, and equipment were paid for by the foundation. Eva attended these events as often as she could. At one event, she explained why she treated children so well. "If we spread all our love on the children to make them really happy, tomorrow we'd have good and grateful adults, and they would become the people of the future. They would be the future leaders of our government, and they'd have a past to be thankful for. They'd be fair, dignified, and generous."[36] Eva understood that a person's childhood shaped the man or woman he or she became.

MONEY AND POWER

In spite of all the good Eva's foundation accomplished, the organization's actions still raised many questions. Millions of

ARGENTINA'S POLICLINICS

Between Perón's inauguration in 1946 and Eva's death in 1952, Argentina's government and Eva's foundation added 45,000 more hospital beds. Many of these beds were located in modern hospitals called policlinics. One of the first policlinics opened in 1947. It was called the Policlinico Presidente Perón and boasted 600 beds. The policlinic had five wings with six floors in each. It also featured an emergency room, several operating rooms, a pharmacy, a library, spacious waiting rooms and terraces, conference rooms, and a special wing for pediatric patients.

Eva Perón visits a children's home in 1947. Although Eva was committed to helping the underclass and countless needy families, questions arose regarding the ethics of her foundation.

dollars poured into the foundation, but the money was never counted or kept track of. Eva's explanation for this was that she didn't have time to account for the money because she was too busy using it to help others. She also called bookkeeping capitalistic nonsense. This attitude, plus the fact that Eva was often seen wearing designer clothing, fabulous fur coats, and expensive jewelry, made many people wonder if she and her husband were putting some of the donations into their own pockets.

Because the foundation was run by the government, Eva did not have to account for any of the money her foundation received or spent. Author Mary Main, who was highly critical of Eva and Perónism, stated that, "In 1949, Congress voted the Foundation fourteen million dollars; and Eva was as free to spend the money as if it were her own pocket money. No accounting whatsoever was required of her; she could spend, invest, donate, or will the funds of the Eva Perón Foundation where she chose."[37]

People also felt that Eva used the foundation to make herself more popular and well-known. Stores and pharmacies run by the foundation were filled with goods that ordinary businesses could not get, such as leather shoes and certain drugs. The press, which was largely controlled by Perón's government, was filed with stories about families who were helped by the foundation. In 1948, posters appeared around Buenos Aires, showing Eva with her arms around two children and the slogan, "Maria Eva Duarte de Perón Brings Happiness to All Homes. Argentines—Uphold Her!"[38]

Perhaps the most disturbing sign of Eva's power was the fact that because her foundation worked in the areas of health care and education, Eva gained control of two government departments: the Department of Public Health and the Ministry of Education. Controlling these departments meant that all the hospitals, schools, and pharmacies in Argentina were under Eva's command, and she could do whatever she wanted with their resources. Her position also gave Eva the power to put companies out of business and clamp down on freedom of speech in the nation's universities.

Critics also accused Eva of brainwashing young children by insisting that schools teach Perónist propaganda. Author

Mary Main, who lived in Argentina during Perónism, reported that textbooks contained lessons extolling Perón and his works, and picture books and magazines were now filled with "good little Perónistas wanting to know why life had suddenly become so beautiful. . . . In a magazine called *Mundo Perónista* . . . in the issue for November 1, 1951—an issue reserved in its entirety for Perónista propaganda—the children's page is dedicated to the Perónista Kid, who is urged to reflect upon the life of General Perón and reminded that a good little Perónista kid is always loyal and brave, and warned, lest he go astray, always to do as General Perón and the Señora Eva Perón do."[39]

Had Eva and Juan Perón become too powerful? Was Argentina a paradise or was it a country facing serious problems because of its government? Those questions were soon on the minds of many people as events began to spiral out of control.

8

The End

When Eva and Juan Perón came to power in 1945, Argentina seemed to be facing a bright and prosperous future. However, in just five years, the state of the country had changed dramatically. By the dawn of the 1950s, Argentina—and Perón's government—faced serious troubles.

A FALTERING ECONOMY

In 1945, Argentina had a surplus of money and goods. The nation was able to lend money to countries around the world and also sell its bounty of meat and grain to nations in Europe. By 1950, Argentina was no longer in a position to lend money to other nations. Instead, it was a nation in debt. In 1950, the United States loaned Argentina $125 million. That still wasn't enough to help Argentina's people buy what they needed.

The cost of living had gone up at an alarming rate. Mary Main stated that "Perón's policy of industrializing a fundamentally rural country . . . is bringing to ruin a nation that was potentially one of the richest in the world."[40] She described how scarce and expensive food had become in Buenos Aires in the early 1950s. "Now milk is bought by the cupful—and some days cannot be bought at all—and *coima* must be paid to the butcher before he will produce a good piece of steak in a city where, ten years ago, tenderloin could be bought for fifteen cents a pound and pasteurized milk was four and a half cents a quart."[41]

By 1951, food was being rationed in Buenos Aires. For example, only half a pound of coffee could be bought at a time. In 1952, Perón asked people to observe one meatless day a week and later requested two meatless days a week. This strategy was shocking in a nation that produced herds of beef cattle and whose people ate more meat than any other nation in the world.

Perón also had an ill-fated scheme to take land away from wealthy landowners and distribute it to workers. He raised taxes extraordinarily high to force owners to give up their land—and sometimes just took the land outright. However, tenant farmers could not afford to pay anyone to work the land nor could they afford the expensive machinery that would do the work for them. As a result, although living conditions improved in the cities, many poor people in rural areas had even less money and fewer prospects than they did before Perón came to power.

Many laborers headed to the big cities to find work rather than stay in rural areas, further depleting the workforce. This led to a sharp decrease in the number of cattle being raised. According to some political parties who opposed Perón, the number of cattle declined by at least 10 million between 1946 and 1949.

THE PERÓNS AS DICTATORS

Financial conditions were not the only things that worried people in Argentina and observers around the world. By 1950, it was clear that Juan Perón had become a dictator, and Eva was right beside him. The government had taken control of just about all the media in the country. The newspapers and radio stations were censored, and they broadcast or printed only the news the Peróns wanted people to hear. Perón and Eva also controlled all the departments and ministries in Argentina, giving them total control over what people could eat, wear, and purchase.

The Peróns also had total control over businesses. Companies who did not contribute to the foundation or do what Eva asked found themselves heavily fined or had their licenses revoked. People who spoke out against the government could be fined, arrested, or jailed.

Eva also continued her strident, often vindictive persecution against members of the upper class. Perón did pretty much whatever Eva asked him to, and she often demanded that he imprison someone for a minor offense that would have been completely overlooked had it been committed by a member of the working class.

Perhaps the most unnerving sign that Perónism had turned into a dictatorship was Eva's ferocious and constant defense of her husband and his policies. In one radio broadcast after another, she demanded nothing less than Argentina's total devotion and faith in Perón and set herself up as a shining example everyone should follow. "My life for Perón!" she proclaimed. "I never wanted anything for myself. My glory is my country's flag."[42] In another address, she cried, "Perón is everything. He is the soul, the nerve, the hope and the reality of the Argentine people. We know that there is only one man here in our movement with his own source of light and that is Perón. We all feed from his light."[43]

People in other nations watched what was going on in Argentina with growing concern and puzzlement. On the surface, things seemed fine. American writer Philip Hamburger visited Buenos Aires in 1948. He noted that, "One does not encounter in Buenos Aires today the orthodox trappings of a

Eva Perón greets the crowds from the balcony of Government House in Buenos Aires. The couple that had begun as advocates for the people had become dictators, even as they remained beloved by many Argentines. By 1951, Eva's supporters were begging her to run as Juan's vice president.

dictatorship. There are no restrictions on travel; people move about freely. . . . There are no concentration camps, and, as far as a stranger can make out, no political prisoners."[44] However, members of Argentina's opposition saw the dangers lurking beneath the surface. One lawyer described Perón as being "subtle, devious, charming. He does not come out into the open and crack skulls. . . . He does his work quietly and cynically. You see, there is so little we can put our hands on these days—everything he does is in the name of 'democracy' and 'social betterment'—and yet we sense the smell of evil in the air, and the thin ledge on which we walk."[45]

VICE PRESIDENT EVA?

Despite the difficult times, the Peróns still had the support of the labor unions and the descamisados. Eva was so popular that many workers and labor unions demanded she run on Perón's political ticket as vice president in the 1951 election.

Other Argentines were not as excited by the idea of Eva as vice president. No woman had ever held such a high office before. Even more unnerving, if anything happened to Perón, Eva would automatically succeed him and become president. This idea was shocking and even offensive for most Argentines.

Perón himself was not sure that having Eva as his running mate would be a wise idea. He knew that Eva made many of his fellow army officers nervous and, after what happened to him in 1945, he could not have forgotten how important the support of the army was to staying in power. However, Perón also knew how much the working class loved Eva and probably

A WOMAN LEADER?

Although the world has seen a number of female rulers in the years since Eva Perón, during the 1950s, it was almost unheard of for a woman to rule a country. Only monarchies in some nations boasted queens, and in many of these nations, queens were only figureheads with no real political power. Argentina's women had only won the right to vote four years earlier, so it was quite shocking for people to think that a woman might be elected vice president.

Ironically, 23 years after Eva Perón considered running for vice president, Juan Perón's third wife, Isabel, would become the first elected female leader in the Western Hemisphere.

believed that having her on the ticket would increase support for himself as well. Whatever his true feelings, Perón allowed Eva's name to be printed on his campaign posters and did not give any hint that she should forget the idea of becoming vice president. In fact, Perón was well aware of his wife's popularity among the masses and once told an aide, "The only person who can stage a popular revolution and overthrow me is my wife."[46]

What no one knew at this time was that Eva was very sick. In 1950, Eva had had her appendix removed, and at that time, doctors discovered that she had uterine cancer. The public was not told about this, and historians aren't sure if Eva herself was told the truth at that time. As Eva began to look weaker and paler in public, her condition was blamed on overwork or anemia. Even when she was wracked with pain, Eva refused to give up her punishing work schedule. She got up early, met with the public, and did her other work all day long. She often did not get back home until after 10 or 11 o'clock at night.

On August 22, 1951, a huge rally was held in front of the Casa Rosada. Unions hired buses to bring thousands of descamisados into the center of the city to proclaim their desire that Eva run for vice president. A huge stage backed with 60-foot-high (18 meters) portraits of Perón and Eva was hastily set up. By nightfall, a crowd estimated at more than a million people jammed the square. They roared with excitement when Perón and Eva took the stage at around five o'clock.

Eva spoke fervently, often interrupted by shouts from the crowd urging her to run for vice president. At last she said, "I shall always do what the people wish, but I tell you, just as I said five years ago, that I would rather be Evita than the wife of the President, if this Evita could do anything for the pain of my country; and so now I say I would rather be Evita."[47]

The crowd, thinking that Eva was refusing to run, called her back to the microphone. Eva returned and begged them to give her four days to make a decision. The crowd shouted back, "No!" At the same time, arguments broke out between Perón and his aides, who were standing beside Eva on the stage. No one had expected the rally to turn in this direction.

Finally, Eva returned to the microphone and said simply, "Friends, as General Perón has said, I will do as the people say."[48] No one was quite sure whether she was accepting or declining the offer, but the crowd peacefully left the square.

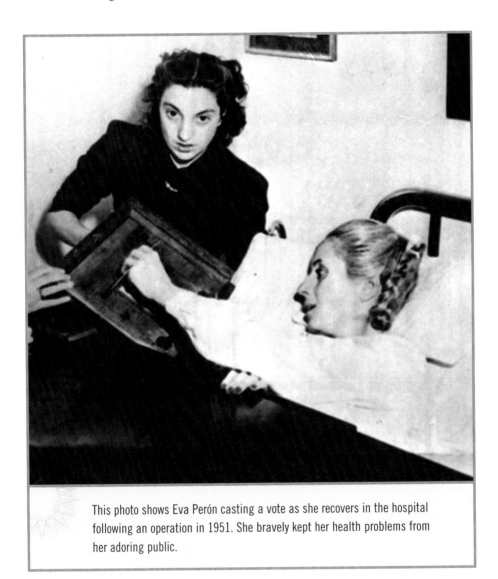

This photo shows Eva Perón casting a vote as she recovers in the hospital following an operation in 1951. She bravely kept her health problems from her adoring public.

On August 31, however, Eva announced in a radio address that she would not run for vice president. Once again, she professed that all she wished to do was serve the people and be a connection between them and her beloved husband. "I only had and, at this moment, I have only one ambition: that it be said in the history books, there was a woman next to Perón who took to the President the hopes of the people, who the people affectionately called Evita."[49]

Historians have debated why Eva and Perón seemed to favor the idea of her as vice president, only to change their minds at the last minute. Eva may well have wanted the title as another sign of how powerful and influential she had become. Or perhaps she only pretended to think about running for vice president, knowing that turning down the job would make her look selfless and continue the myth that she would sacrifice anything for the good of Perón and her country.

EVA'S LAST ILLNESS

Whatever Eva's motivations, it soon became clear that she could never serve as vice president. Shortly after the rally, Eva collapsed. Doctors finally told Perón the truth: Eva was dying of uterine cancer. The Peróns' close friend, Father Benitez, was with Perón when he heard the news and recalled that the death sentence hit him hard. "This blow struck Perón as hard as anything he had ever experienced. His life would be entirely altered. He knew exactly what was in store for him the moment he was told, as his first wife, Aurelia, had suffered from the same illness and, after they had tried and failed with every type of treatment, she had died in great pain, which affected him more than her."[50]

Doctors performed surgery to remove the cancer, and the operation seemed to be successful at first. However, just a few months later, Eva's symptoms were back, and doctors discovered that the cancer had returned and was even worse than before.

The crowds noticed that Eva did not appear with Perón or give any speeches, and they demanded to know what was wrong. The government released several statements saying that she was ill but did not give any details or hints of just how serious her conditions was. Nevertheless, people began to hold masses for Eva, praying for her health.

Eva had another operation early in November, shortly before the presidential elections. Before she went into the hospital, she gave a radio broadcast that warned, "Not to vote for Perón is for an Argentine . . . to betray the country."[51] Eva voted for Perón from her hospital bed. To no one's surprise, Perón was re-elected to another term as president.

Eva made a few public appearances over the next few months and surprised her doctors by surviving longer than they had expected. However, even though the doctors lied and told her she was doing better, and even placed weights on her scale to disguise how much weight she was losing, Eva was no longer fooled. She knew she was dying. She told Father Benitez, "You are lying to me as if I were a coward. I know I have fallen into a pit and no one can get me out."[52]

Despite her condition, Eva made several more speeches from the balcony of the Casa Rosada. Her statements became more violent and intense. On May 1, Eva proclaimed her hatred of anyone who opposed Perón. "If it is necessary, we will execute justice with our own hands. I ask God not to allow these madmen to raise their hands against Perón, for beware of the day when I will go down with the working people, I will go down with the women of the people, I will go down with the *descamisados* . . . and I will leave nothing standing that is not for Perón."[53]

Eva's last public appearance was at Perón's second inauguration on June 4, 1952. She rode with him in an open car, but no one knew that she did not have the strength to stand on her own. Instead, her body was held up by a plaster cast hidden under her long fur coat.

EVA'S DEATH

Eva Perón died on July 26, 1952. She was 33 years old. The country went through an outpouring of grief and hysteria that no one had ever seen before. The descamisados were heartbroken. They couldn't believe their beloved Evita was gone. Members of the oligarchy were not upset; on the contrary, they were thrilled. The despised Eva Perón was finally gone.

The government announced an official period of mourning. All business and political activity would cease for two days. There would be 30 days of official mourning. Church bells tolled throughout the country.

For three days, Buenos Aires shut down. Stores and restaurants closed, and no one went to work. The sidewalks and street in front of the Ministry of Labor were buried under a carpet of flowers left in tribute to Eva. People gathered in front of the Ministry of Labor, soon filling the streets for blocks.

Eva's body was prepared and laid out in a glass-topped coffin, which was then put on display in the Ministry of Labor. Crowds of people lined up in the rain, some waiting for days. They marched into the ministry and up a flight of stairs to the coffin. Many people broke down and wept when they saw Eva's body, and foundation nurses stood nearby to help anyone who needed assistance. Although Eva's body was supposed to lie in state for only three days, the crowds were so great that the government extended the period indefinitely. It took more than 13 days for everyone who wanted to see Eva to make it inside, and lines stretched up to 30 blocks long.

Finally, Eva's body was removed and taken to the headquarters of one of the labor unions. Perón wanted to preserve Eva's body forever, so it could be exhibited in its glass coffin. A doctor named Pedro Ara was summoned to do the work in secret. Eva's body disappeared from public view, and the nation tried to come to grips with its loss—and figure out what to do next.

After Evita

Things were changing in Argentina. Around the time of Eva's death, the economy was collapsing and the government was losing control. Eva's death only made things worse, and the country was soon thrown into chaos.

ANOTHER REVOLUTION

At the time of Eva's death, Argentina was in turmoil. Two bad harvests had drastically cut the country's production of wheat, and the cattle industry was also in decline. A beef shortage meant that meat could barely be found, and what little there was had such a high price that many people could not afford to buy it. In time, beef could be bought only on the black market at outrageous prices.

Perón's government also used brutal methods to control the people. Perón's security forces swooped down and arrested anyone who spoke out against Perón or his policies. Offenders were jailed and tortured.

The government also faced a number of scandals. One involved Eva's brother, Juan Duarte, who had served as Perón's secretary for years. Duarte was accused of dealing in beef on the black market. When Perón demanded an investigation in 1953, Duarte killed himself. Rumors swirled that Perón had actually had Duarte murdered in order to cover up even worse scandals.

In 1955, Perón still had the support of the labor unions and the Catholic Church, but that year he confronted the church's power. Perón eliminated many religious holidays, legalized divorce (which was against Catholic teaching), and no longer required schools to teach Catholicism. The clergy and many devout Catholics rose up against Perón and staged a huge demonstration in front of a cathedral in Buenos Aires. Later, several churches were stoned and burned in retaliation. It was a fatal mistake on Perón's part.

Perón's persecution of the church made many people in the armed forces nervous. On June 16, 1955, a squadron of naval aircraft bombed the Casa Rosada. The bombs missed their target and several hundred people in the streets were killed. Another naval unit attacked the Casa Rosada. Perón was not there at the time, but many of his supporters were killed.

Once the military and the church turned against Perón, his days were numbered. Even the working class and the labor unions could no longer support him, now that the country's financial crisis made it impossible for Perón to fund the labor unions and give out raises as he had in the past. Perón also could not continue the work of Eva's foundation or give it the personal attention that she had. Although he went to the foundation's offices a few times to meet with the poor, Perón soon stopped coming, expressing his amazement that Eva could do that work day after day.

Hunderds of thousands of mourners light the way for a parade staged in memory of Eva Perón. Evita was a highly polarizing figure whose death greatly impacted Argentina and much of the world.

It was also clear that Perón had lost his touch with people. Colonel Pablo Vicente said, "Evita was truly a bridge between Perón and his people. Her death caused him to lose contact with the people and with Argentina's everyday reality."[54] On September 20, 1955, just three years after Eva's death, the army seized power and sent Perón into exile in Spain.

EVITA: SAINT OR DEVIL?

During the chaos in the two years after her death, legends about Eva spread like wildfire throughout Argentina. Some people viewed her as a saint, their "Santa Evita." Just one month after her death, the newspaper vendors' union suggested that the Vatican make her a saint, and in 1953, they published a calendar featuring a drawing of Eva dressed in blue robes like the Virgin Mary, her head surrounded by a halo. Although the Vatican never took the request for sainthood seriously, many Argentines did view Eva as holy. Perón's government encouraged this by publishing prayers and devotional literature in her name. One book used by schoolchildren to learn to read included this prayer:

> Our little Mother, thou who art in heaven,
> Good fairy laughing amongst the angels . . .
> Evita, I promise to be as good as you wish me to be,
> Respecting God, loving my country;
> Taking care of General Perón; studying
> And being towards everyone the child
> You dreamed I would be; healthy, happy,
> Well-educated and pure in heart.[55]

Cities, schools, and subway stations were renamed after Eva. The government also built statues of her and issued stamps with Eva's picture on them. The time of the evening news broadcast was even changed from 8:30 to 8:25, because that was the exact time Eva had died.

Other people had a completely different view of Eva. She had always had enemies in the upper classes, and after Perón's overthrow in 1955, this segment of the population began to spread entirely different rumors about Eva. They claimed that she had used donations from the foundation for her own good, spending the money on clothes and jewelry for herself. They also claimed she had hidden millions

EVA PERÓN'S PLACE IN HISTORY

For many years after Perón was forced out of office in 1955, Eva was seen as evil and the government did not allow anyone to talk about her or her husband. After Perón returned briefly to power in the early 1970s, Eva once again became a symbol of the country and its glory days during the 1940s. Even after Perón died and his third wife, Isabel, was forced out of power, people remained fascinated with Evita. The government released more information about her, opening its archives and releasing texts of her speeches and allowing people to visit her burial site. The young people of Argentina, who had been born after Eva died, learned about her and began to see her as something more than a symbol. In time, it became clear that Eva was not a devil or a saint, but an important political figure who helped shape Argentina's government and the events of the 1940s and 1950s.

Eva Perón has been dead for almost 60 years, yet she still has a powerful hold over the people of Argentina. Her image was still used by political candidates in their campaigns for decades after her death. In 2002, Hilda de Duhalde, wife of Argentine president Eduardo Duhalde, was often compared favorably to Eva Perón because she was frequently seen at her husband's side and was an important figure in his government.

Eva's rise to power also caused changes to Argentina's political system that are still felt today. Eva was instrumental in winning the right to vote for women. Since her death, Argentina's women have continued to gain a great deal of political power. In 2007, Cristina Fernandez de Kirchner was elected president of Argentina. She was the first elected female president in Argentina's history. Today, female leaders and women with great political power are fairly common all over the world, which is a big change since Eva's time, when her presence was viewed with suspicion and disgust.

Argentina still faces many problems, and its history of unstable governments seems to be an everyday fact of life. Eva Perón was such a powerful figure that it is likely her image and life will always be a presence in Argentina, no matter what direction the future may take there.

of dollars and jewels in European bank accounts during her Rainbow Tour.

After Perón's exile, the government tried to wipe away all traces of Eva. She was no longer talked about in schools. It became a crime to possess photographs of Eva or Perón, and Perón's political party was disbanded. Eva's name was even cut out of sheets used in foundation hospitals and homes. On July 4, 1956, the government officially took over the foundation and transferred all of its assets into the national treasury. The government also issued a statement that the foundation had been used "for political corruption and acts of favouritism that by themselves constitute the denial of any healthy concept of social justice."[56]

EVA'S BODY

Even Eva's body was not safe from the chaos that raged through Argentina. After her death, Eva's body had been taken to a hidden location where it was preserved by Dr. Pedro Ara. Although the location was supposed to be a secret, it did not take long for the public to figure out where Eva's body was. Soon candles, photos of Eva, and bouquets of flowers were being left outside the gates. The government did not know what to do. It feared that if Eva's body was buried in Argentina, her tomb would become a shrine and a rallying point for another revolution.

President Pedro Arambaru and the ruling members considered cremating, or burning, Eva's body, but this procedure was against the rules of the Catholic Church. Although some of his advisors wanted the body destroyed anyway, President Arambaru was a devout Catholic and refused to even consider the idea. Finally, he and his advisers decided that Eva's body should be taken out of the country and buried somewhere else in secret.

In 1957, Colonel Hector Cabanillas of Argentina's Army Intelligence and several priests arranged for Eva's body to be shipped to Italy. Eva was buried in a grave under the name

Maria Maggi. President Arambaru and his advisers asked not to be told any of the details, so they could truthfully say that they knew nothing about the whereabouts of Eva's body.

Many years later, after years of political turmoil, Perónism was no longer viewed as entirely evil by Argentina's government. Juan Perón was still in exile in Spain, and he was asked if he would like his wife's body. He said yes, and in September 1971, Eva's body was moved from Italy to Spain and given to Perón to rebury in a Spanish cemetery.

THE RETURN OF JUAN PERÓN

By 1973, Argentina had seen five military and three civilian governments. Prices were still high, and violence, repression, and corruption were still standard practices. Finally, in 1973, Argentina's military government allowed free elections. Juan Perón ran for president and he won. Showing a cynical sense of humor, Perón commented about his victory: "It was not that we were so good, but those who followed us were so bad it made us look better than we were."[57]

By this time, Perón was married to his third wife, Isabel. The couple returned to Argentina, where Isabel announced that she hoped to follow in Evita's footsteps. She often held up photos of Eva during speeches and led chants celebrating Eva from the balcony of the Casa Rosada.

Nostalgia for Eva Perón was running high during this time, and Isabel became a substitute for Eva. Although she lacked Eva's passion and skill at public speaking, Isabel achieved what Eva was denied. In 1974, she ran for vice president on the ticket with her husband as president. The Perón ticket won. Then, on July 1, 1974, Perón died of pneumonia and a heart attack just nine months after taking office. Isabel became the president of Argentina and the first non-royal female head of state in the Western Hemisphere. In 1976, she had Eva's body shipped to Argentina, where it was finally buried in the Duarte family's tomb in Buenos Aires.

EVA ON STAGE AND SCREEN

Eva Perón continued to fascinate people decades after her death. In 1978, the musical *Evita* opened in London. *Evita* was written by the immensely popular team of Tim Rice and Andrew Lloyd Webber, and it opened to excellent reviews. The show was a huge success. It moved from London to Broadway and eventually played in cities around the world. *Evita* ran for more than seven years and earned an estimated $1 billion.

Evita was based on some of the more negative accounts of Eva's life, and it included most of the vicious gossip that had followed her for years. However, Rice and Webber also showed the public's devotion for their "Santa Evita." Rice and Webber also introduced the character of real-life revolutionary Che

THE THIRD SEÑORA PERÓN

Isabel Perón was born in 1931. Like Eva, she started her career in the entertainment industry, working as a dancer. Isabel gave up show business when she met Juan Perón in 1955. She became Perón's personal secretary and accompanied him into exile in Madrid, Spain. The couple married in 1961. During her husband's exile, Isabel visited Argentina several times during the 1960s and early 1970s to build support for him. They returned to Argentina in 1973.

Isabel became the first woman president in the Americas when she succeeded Perón in 1974. However, she was an ineffective and unpopular leader whose rule was plagued by economic problems, government corruption, political violence, and labor union unrest. On March 24, 1976, she was overthrown by a military coup. After five years of house arrest, she was exiled to Spain in 1981. In 2007, an Argentine judge issued an arrest warrant for Isabel for allowing the military to commit human rights abuses during her rule. Isabel remains in Spain, out of reach of Argentina's court system.

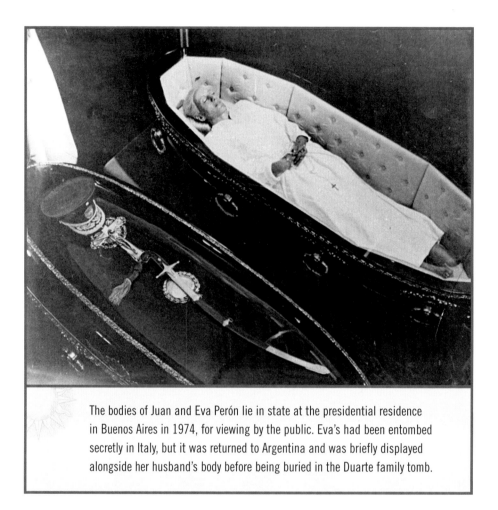

The bodies of Juan and Eva Perón lie in state at the presidential residence in Buenos Aires in 1974, for viewing by the public. Eva's had been entombed secretly in Italy, but it was returned to Argentina and was briefly displayed alongside her husband's body before being buried in the Duarte family tomb.

Guevara. Although there is no evidence that Guevara and Eva ever met, his presence in the show allowed the writers to show a counterpoint to the public's adoration of Evita.

In 1996, the stage version of *Evita* was turned into a movie of the same name. Pop star Madonna begged for and eventually won the role of Eva. Che Guevara was played by Spanish actor Antonio Banderas, and Juan Perón was played by British actor Jonathan Pryce. The movie was very successful and was nominated for five Academy Awards, winning one award for Best Song. Both the stage version and the movie reignited interest in Eva Perón, and stories about her life appeared regularly in the news at that time.

Today, more than 50 years after her death, historians still debate who Eva Perón really was and what she meant to Argentina. Was she a saint or evil incarnate? Did she truly want to help others or was she only interested in increasing the fortunes of herself and her husband? Perhaps the answer is yes to all of these questions. As her friend Father Hernan Benitez told an interviewer during the 1980s, "She left behind tremendous mistakes, but also tremendous successes."[58] The world may never know who Eva Perón truly was, but she continues to fascinate people to this day.

Chronology

1919   Eva Duarte is born in Los Toldos, Argentina,
       on May 7.

1920   Eva's father, Juan Duarte, leaves the family.

1926   Juan Duarte is killed in a car crash on January 8.

1930   Eva's family moves to Junin.

1935   Eva moves to Buenos Aires to pursue a career in radio
       and acting.

1944   Eva meets Juan Perón at a benefit on January 22.

1945   Juan Perón is forced to resign from the government and
       is imprisoned; a general strike on October 17 frees him;
       Perón and Eva marry on October 22.

1946   Eva becomes Argentina's First Lady when her husband is
       elected president on June 5.

1919
Eva Duarte
is born in
Los Toldos,
Argentina, on
May 7

1935
Eva moves to
Buenos Aires
to pursue
a career in
radio and
acting

1945
Perón and Eva marry
on October 22

1919

1945

1926
Juan Duarte
is killed in a
car crash on
January 8

1944
Eva meets Juan Perón at
a benefit on January 22

1947   Eva goes on her Rainbow Tour of Europe.

1948   Eva founds the Eva Perón Foundation on June 19.

1950   Eva is diagnosed with uterine cancer, but the news is kept secret from the public.

1951   Labor unions rally on August 22 and demand Eva run for vice president; she declines the offer on August 31.

1952   Eva makes her last public appearance at her husband's second inauguration on June 4; she dies in Buenos Aires on July 26.

1955   Juan Perón is deposed and exiled.

1957   Eva's body is secretly buried in Italy.

1971   Eva's body is moved to Spain, where Juan Perón is living in exile.

1946
Eva becomes Argentina's First Lady

1950
Eva is diagnosed with uterine cancer, but the news is kept secret from the public

1976
Isabel Perón has Eva's body moved to Argentina, where it is buried in the Duarte family tomb

1946   1976

1948
Eva founds the Eva Perón Foundation on June 19

1952
Eva makes her last public appearance at her husband's second inauguration on June 4; she dies in Buenos Aires on July 26

1973 Juan Perón returns to power in Argentina.

1974 Perón dies on July 1 and his wife, Isabel, becomes Argentina's president.

1976 Isabel Perón has Eva's body moved to Argentina, where it is buried in the Duarte family tomb.

Notes

Chapter One

1 Quoted in Dolane Larson, translator, "To Be Evita, Part I." Eva Perón Historical Research Foundation. www.evitaPerón.org/part1.htm. April 5, 2009.

2 Ibid.

3 Mary Main, *Evita: The Woman with the Whip*. New York: Dodd, Mead & Company, 1980, pp. 22–23.

Chapter Two

4 Quoted in Nicholas Fraser and Marysa Navarro, *Evita: The Real Life of Eva Perón*. New York: W.W. Norton Company, 1996, p. 5.

5 Interview with Palmira Repetti, quoted in Fraser and Navarro, *Evita: The Real Life of Eva Perón*, p. 8.

6 Quoted in Fraser and Navarro, *Evita: The Real Life of Eva Perón*, p. 10.

Chapter Three

7 Blanca Duarte de Alvarez Rodriguez, "Bianca Duarte: Our True Life." Eva Person Historical Research Foundation. www.evitaPerón.org/mens.htm. May 15, 2009.

8 Ibid.

9 Ibid.

10 Quoted in Tulio Demicheli, *The Mystery of Eva Perón: The True Story of Evita*. DVD. New York: First Run Features, 1987.

11 Quoted in Fraser and Navarro, *Evita: The Real Life of Eva Perón*, p. 21.

Chapter Four

12 Quoted in Fraser and Navarro, *Evita: The Real Life of Eva Perón*, p. 33.

13 Ibid.

14 Quoted in Main, *Evita: The Woman with the Whip*, p. 58.

15 Quoted in Fraser and Navarro, *Evita: The Real Life of Eva Perón*, p. 43.

Chapter Five

16 Quoted in Fraser and Navarro, *Evita: The Real Life of Eva Perón*, p. 59.

17 Quoted in *The Mystery of Eva Perón: The True Story of Evita*.

18 Quoted in Fraser and Navarro, *Evita: The Real Life of Eva Perón*, p. 66.

19 Ibid, p. 67.

20 Quoted in *The Mystery of Eva Perón: The True Story of Evita*.

21 Ibid.

22 Quoted in Dolane Larson, translator, "To Be Evita, Part II." Eva Perón Historical Research Foundation. www.evitaPerón.org/part1.htm. April 5, 2009.

Chapter Six

23 Quoted in *The Mystery of Eva Perón: The True Story of Evita*.

24 Quoted in Fraser and Navarro, *Evita: The Real Life of Eva Perón*, p. 85.

25 Quoted in Dolane Larson, translator, "To Be Evita, Part II."

26 Ibid.

27 Quoted in Fraser and Navarro, *Evita: The Real Life of Eva Perón*, p. 85.

28 Quoted in *The Mystery of Eva Perón: The True Story of Evita*.

29 Ibid.

Chapter Seven

30 Fraser and Navarro, *Evita: The Real Life of Eva Perón*, p. 115.

31 Quoted in *The Mystery of Eva Perón: The True Story of Evita*.

32 Quoted in Fraser and Navarro, *Evita: The Real Life of Eva Perón*, p. 117.

33 Quoted in Noemi Castineiras, "Eva Perón Foundation From Its

Beginnings to the Death of Evita." Eva Perón Historical Research Foundation. www.evitaPerón.org/f0.htm. May 15, 2009.

34 Quoted in *The Mystery of Eva Perón: The True Story of Evita.*

35 Quoted in Dolane Larson, "Eva Perón Foundation: Health and Safety Net—Policlinics." Eva Perón Historical Research Foundation. www.evitaPerón.org/health_eva_Perón.htm. May 15, 2009.

36 Quoted in *The Mystery of Eva Perón: The True Story of Evita.*

37 Mary Main, *Evita: The Woman with the Whip*, p. 196.

38 Ibid, p. 198.

39 Ibid, p. 206.

Chapter Eight

40 Mary Main, *Evita: The Woman with the Whip*, p. 140.

41 Ibid, p. 140.

42 Quoted in *The Mystery of Eva Perón: The True Story of Evita.*

43 Quoted in Fraser and Navarro, *Evita: The Real Life of Eva Perón*, p. 112.

44 Ibid, p. 102.

45 Ibid, p. 102.

46 Quoted in *The Mystery of Eva Perón: The True Story of Evita.*

47 Ibid.

48 Quoted in Dolane Larson, translator, "Eva Perón Biography." Eva Perón Historical Research Foundation. www.evitaPerón.org/part3.htm. July 11, 2009.

49 Quoted in *The Mystery of Eva Perón: The True Story of Evita.*

50 Quoted in Fraser and Navarro, *Evita: The Real Life of Eva Perón*, p. 148.

51 Quoted in Mary Main, *Evita: The Woman with the Whip*, p. 279.

52 Quoted in Fraser and Navarro, *Evita: The Real Life of Eva Perón*, p. 159.

53 Ibid, p. 155.

Chapter Nine

54 Quoted in *The Mystery of Eva Perón: The True Story of Evita.*

55 Quoted in Fraser and Navarro, *Evita: The Real Life of Eva Perón*, p. 170.

56 Ibid, p. 178.

57 Quoted in Mary Main, *Evita: The Woman with the Whip*, p. 283.

58 Quoted in *The Mystery of Eva Perón: The True Story of Evita.*

Bibliography

Books

Fraser, Nicholas, and Marysa Navarro. *Evita: The Real Life of Eva Perón*. New York: W.W. Norton and Company, 1996.

Main, Mary. *Evita: The Woman with the Whip*. New York: Dodd, Mead and Company, 1980.

Perón, Eva. *My Mission in Life*. New York: Vantage Press, 1952.

Plotkin, Mariano Ben. *Manana es San Perón: A Cultural History of Perón's Argentina*. Wilmington, Del.: Scholarly Resources, 2003.

Taylor, J.M. *Eva Perón: The Myths of a Woman*. Chicago: University of Chicago Press, 1979.

DVDs

Demicheli, Tulio. *The Mystery of Eva Perón: The True Story of Evita*. New York: First Run Features, 1987.

Web Sites

Biography.com. "Isabel Perón Biography." Retrieved July 21, 2009. http://www.biography.com/articles/Isabel_Per%C3%B3n-39252.

Castineiras, Noemi. "Eva Perón Foundation From Its Beginnings to the Death of Evita." Eva Perón Historical Research Foundation. Retrieved July 11, 2009. http://www.evitaPerón.org/f0.htm.

Duarte, Blanca. "Our True Life." Evita Perón Historical Research Foundation. December 1997. Retrieved May 15, 2009. http://www.evitaPerón.org/mens.htm.

Encyclopedia of the Nations. "Argentina—Labor." Retrieved July 21, 2009. http://www.nationsencyclopedia.com/Americas/Argentina-LABOR.html.

Frommer's. "Casa Rosada and the Presidential Museum." Retrieved July 21, 2009. http://www.frommers.com/destinations/buenosaires/A34239.html.

Larson, Dolane. "Eva Perón Foundation." Evita Perón Historical Research Foundation. Retrieved May 15, 2009. http://www.evitaPerón.org/f0.htm.

Larson, Dolane. "Evita: Actress." Evita Perón Historical Research Foundation. Retrieved May 15, 2009. http://www.evitaPerón.org/actr1.htm.

Larson, Dolane. "Eva Perón Foundation: Health and Safety Net—Policlinics." Eva Perón Historical Research Foundation. Retrieved May 15, 2009. http://www.evitaPerón.org/health_eva_Perón.htm.

Larson, Dolane. "To Be Evita." Evita Perón Historical Research Foundation. Retrieved April 5, 2009. http://www.evitaPerón.org/part1.htm.

Lewis, Robert. "Juan and Eva Perón: Exploring a Legacy of Political Immortality." Associated Content. February 26, 2008. Retrieved August 2, 2009. http://www.associatedcontent.com/article/618475/juan-and-eva-Perón-exploring-a-legacy.html?cat=49.

Minster, Christopher. "The History of Buenos Aires." About.com. Retrieved July 21, 2009. http://latinamericanhistory.about.com/od/historyofsouthamerica/a/buenosaires.htm.

Moore, Don. "Radio with a Past in Argentina." Patepluma Radio: International Radio Homepage. January 1995. Retrieved July 21, 2009. http://www.pateplumaradio.com/south/misc/argendx.html.

Richman, Sheldon. "Fascism." The Concise Encyclopedia of Economics. Library of Economics and Liberty. Retrieved July 21, 2009. http://www.econlib.org/library/Enc/Fascism.html.

Rohter, Larry. "In Footsteps of Evita: Argentina's New First Lady." New York Times. February 1, 2002. Retrieved August 2, 2009. http://www.nytimes.com/2002/02/01/world/in-footsteps-of-evita-argentina-s-new-first-lady.html?pagewanted=all.

Further Reading

Books

Fearns, Les, and Daisy Fearns. *Argentina*. New York: Facts On File, 2005.

Shields, Charles. *Argentina*. Philadelphia: Mason Crest Publishers, 2005.

Spengler, Kremena. *Eva Perón: First Lady of the People*. Mankato, Minn.: Capstone Press, 2007.

Stille, Darlene R. *Eva Perón: First Lady of Argentina*. Minneapolis, Minn.: Compass Point Books, 2006.

Web Sites

Encyclopedia of World Biography. "Eva Perón Biography." Retrieved June 5, 2009. http://www.notablebiographies.com/Pe-Pu/Per-n-Eva.htm.)

Portland State University. "People Who Have Changed the World: Eva Perón." Retrieved June 28, 2009. http://www.wc.pdx.edu/evitaPerón/.

Picture Credits

page:

Index

Page numbers in *italics* indicate photos or illustrations.

A

acting *18*, 22–30, 36. See also Movies
Agrupación Radial Argentina 37
appendicitis 73
Ara, Pedro 83
Arambaru, Pedro 83
Argentina, geography of 9
arrests 40–43, 78–79
Arrieta (Major) 29

B

Banderas, Antonio 86
Beneficent Society 59–62
Benitez, Herman 45, 60, 75, 76, 87
Biographies of Illustrious Women 28, 36
birth of Eva Péron 8–9
black myth 8
body, fate of 77, 83–84, *86*
brainwashing 66–67
bribery 10
brutality 78–79
Buenos Aires 26

C

La Cabalgata del Circo 36
Cabanillas, Hector 83
cancer 6, 33, 73, 75–77
candombe 24
Casa Rosada 43, 44, 73, 79
Castillo, Ramón 29
Catholic Church 37, 79, 83
cattle 69, 78
censorship 70
CGT. See Confederación General del Trabajo
charity

Beneficent Society and 59–62
Eva Péron Foundation and 62–64, 70, 79
questions surrounding 64–67, *65*
children 64, *65*
class structure, overview of 53
Company of the Theater of the Air 28
Confederación General del Trabajo (CGT) 34
cooking 17

D

dancing 24–25
Dancing with the Stars 25
death of Eva Péron 6–8, *7*, *11*, 77
debt 68–69
Department of Public Health 66
El Descaisado 47
dictatorship 69–72
divorce 79
The Divorcee 19
donations, mandatory 62
Duarte, Blanca (sister) 9, 14, 17
Duarte, Elisa (sister) 9, 14, 17, 29
Duarte, Erminda (sister) 9, 12, 14, 21, 22
Duarte, Juan (brother) 9, 14, 17, 53, 79
Duarte, Juan (father) 9–11, 14–15
Duhalde, Eduardo 82
Duhalde, Hilda de 82

E

earthquake 31–33
economy 48–49, 68–69
education 14, 17, 66
Elsa (friend) 17, 20
entertainment 60

Eva Péron Foundation 62–64, 70, 79
Evita 85–86
exile 80, 85

F

factory owners 49–50
Farrell, Edelmiro 33, 39, 40
Fascism 54, 56
Fernandez de Kirchner, Cristina 82
food scarcity 68–69, 78
Forever Tango 25
Franco, Francisco 54, 55, 56
fraud 10
freedom of speech 29

G

Gardel, Carlos 24–25
General Confederation of Labor 34
Ghioldi, Americo 63
glamour 53–54
Grand Cross of Isabella the Catholic 55
Great Britain 57
Grisolia de Duarte, Estela 15
Guevara, Che 85–86
Guibourg, Edmundo 28

H

habanera 24
hair color 36
health care 63–64, 66
Hitler, Adolf 39, 56
housing 52

I

Ibarguren, Juana (mother) 9, 11–12, 14–15
illegitimacy 12
Imbert, Anibal 30
Indians 9
Italy 33, 56

K

Kartulowicz, Emilio 28

L
labor department 33, 36
Labor Party 45–47
labor unions. See Unions
land ownership 49–50,
    69

M
Madonna 86
Magaldi, Agustin 23
Maggi, Maria 84
marriage 41–42, 45
Martin Garcia 41
Mazza, Miguel Angel
    41–42
medical care 63–64, 66
military 29, 32, 39,
    79–80
milonga 24
minister of war posi-
    tion 39
Ministry of Education
    66
movies *18*, 19–20,
    27, 36, 86. See also
    Acting
Mundo Perónista 67
musicals 85–86
Mussolini, Benito 33, 56

N
nationalization 49
navy 41
Nazi Party 39, 56

O
oligarchy 10, 37–39,
    50, 60
orphanages 60

P
pampas 9
Pelliciotta, Pascual 28
Perón, Isabel 72, 82,
    84, 85
Perón, Juan (husband)
    arrest of 40–42
    death of 84
    death of Eva Péron
        and *11*

early relationship with
    32–37
increasing political
    power of 33–37
opposition to 8, 37–39
ousting of 78–80
overview of 32–33
as president 48–49
reelection of 75–76
release of 43–44
return to power of 82,
    84
running for president
    45–47
Perón Foundation
    62–64, 70, 79
Perónist Women's Party
    58
Pius XII (Pope) *55*, 56
Plaza de Mayo 42, 44
pleurisy 42
poetry readings 21, 22,
    24
Policlinico Presidente
    Perón 64
policlinics 64
poverty 12
Prime Arini's Music
    Store 22
prison 41–42
propaganda 29, 36–37,
    66–67
Pryce, Jonathan 86
puchero 13

R
Radical Party 10
Radio Argentina 29
Radio Belgrano 29, 36,
    40
Radio El Mundo 29
Radio Splendid 29
railroads 49
Rainbow Tour 54–57,
    55, 83
Ramirez, Pedro Pablo
    29–30, 39
rationing 69
La Razon de mi Vida
    (Perón) 34–35, 52

revolutions 42–44,
    78–80
Reyes, Cipriano 45
Rice, Tim 85–86
Rodriguez, Jose Alvarez
    23
Roman Catholic Church
    37, 79, 83

S
sainthood 81
San Juan earthquake
    31–33
San Miguel Studios 36
scandals 79
schools 14, 17, 66
sewing 12, 13, 17
Shearer, Norma 19–20
Sintonia 20, 28
social classes, overview
    of 53
Socialism 56
Sociedad de Beneficencia
    59–62
Spain 54, 55, 85
strikes 42

T
tango 24–25
Tango Argentino 25
taxes 69
Thalberg, Irving 19
Tizon, Aurelia 33
torture 39

U
unions
    formation of additional
        49
    revolution and 42–45
    solving problems and
        52
    support of 32, 33, 34,
        37, 79
uterine cancer 6, 33, 73,
    75–77

V
vice presidency 39, *71*,
    72–75, 84

Vicente, Pablo 80
Villa Soldati 52
voting reforms 10,
    57–58, 82, 84

W
Wagner, Richard 29
war minister position 33

Webber, Andrew Lloyd
    85–86
white myth 8
Widow Duarte 17
"The Woman" 36–37
women's suffrage 57–58,
    82
working class 50–53,

51. See also
    Unions
World War II 33, 36,
    48–49, 56

Z
Ziegfield Follies 19
Zucker, Marcus 26–27

About the Author

Joanne Mattern is the author of more than 300 children's books and has also worked as an editor for several major children's publishers. She specializes in nonfiction and especially enjoys writing biographies and books about history and nature. Her goal is to bring the stories of real people and events to life for today's readers. Joanne lives in New York State with her husband, four children, and an assortment of pets.